Printed By

River City Graphic Arts Co.

833 Avenue G   •   Fort Madison, IA 52627
319-372-9069   •   1-800-254-3895

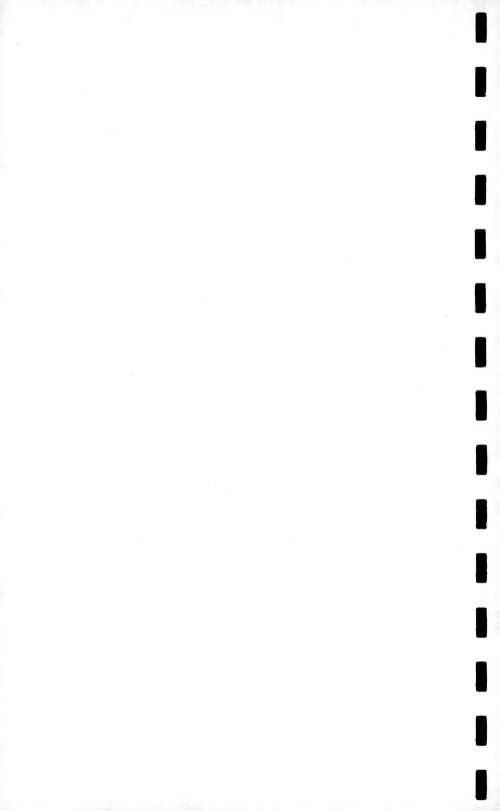

HERBAL COOKERY

by
Dixie L. Stephen

HEARTS 'N TUMMIES COOKBOOK COMPANY
A Dinky Division of Quixote Press

1-800-571-BOOK

The taste, smell and texture of herbs has been woven into our lives since ancient times. Herbs provide a connection to our past – and an enhancement to our present. Writing this book represents, to a certain extent, the fruition of that interconnection. It is you, the reader, who completes the dance. May you more deeply engage in the joy of herbs.

Table of Contents

Harvesting and Preserving Herbs 13
    Drying.. 14
    Freezing.. 16
    Herbed Vinegars 17
    Herbal Infused Oils........................... 19

Stocking Your Spice Cabinet.. 21
    Herb Blends 22
    Pestos.. 25

Beverages... 28

Appetizers 33

Herb Butters and Spreads 37

Salads Dressings and Sauces 45

Vegetables.. 51

Breads 64

Pastas.. 71

Soup 76

Main Dishes.. 81

Meat and Fish... 88

Herbal Jellies.. 104

Desserts.. 106

Pet Pantry 115

Index 119

PREFACE

I have been an avid cook and gardener since childhood.
As a result, the resurgence of herbs in the last decade has
been a joy to behold. Growing and using herbs has been
my avocation for the better part of thirty years. That
interest ultimately became a vocation. For ten of the last
thirteen years, we owned Busha's Brae Herb Farm
located in the rolling hills of Leelanau County in
northwestern Michigan. We sold Busha's Brae in 1994 so
that I could share my passion with others through my
writing.

DEDICATION

*This book is dedicated to my husband Jim,
who would have been so pleased.*

ACKNOWLEDGEMENTS

So many thanks to the terrific people that have helped make this book a reality. A big thank you to Bruce Carlson, the editor and publisher, who kept his foot firmly planted in the middle of my back; and to my family and friends who kept a kindly hand on my shoulder. To Paul, who installed the technology that brought this book to print and me to total frustration.

Cooking is by its nature an experimental task. We have long had a saying in our house: "You have to kiss a lot of frogs to find your prince." I especially want to thank my children, Kent, Chad, David and Anne, and my husband Jim because...they kissed a *lot* of frogs while I perfected these recipes.

HARVESTING AND PRESERVING HERBS

HARVESTING AND PRESERVING HERBS

Fresh-cut herbs are one of the delights of summer. With a minimal amount of planning and effort, most herbs will yield their fragrance and flavor the year around. Whether you have a special herb garden, or a few patio pots with herbs, you have the potential for a winter harvest. Herbs can be dried, frozen, or preserved in pestos, oils and vinegars.

Drying is the age-old method that requires the least amount of special equipment or effort. Simply cut the herbs in the morning after the dew has dried, bundle them with rubber bands and hang in a warm, dry, dark place with good air circulation. Good drying temperatures range between 90 and 110 degrees. I prefer to dry at 100 degrees. If an herb goes into the drying process green, it should be green when it's drying is complete. Careful attention to temperature is a major factor in this process.

Microwave Drying is an excellent way to dry small quantities of herbs. Lay two or three layers of paper towels in the oven, place a single layer of herb stems or individual leaves on the towels. Dry according to your microwave instruction manual, or experiment with time and temperature until you have green, crisp-dry herbs. Use 30-second time cycles. Remove herbs to wire racks in a warm area for a short time before placing in sealed containers in a dark place for storage. Do not crush herbs completely until you are ready to use them.

Convection Oven Drying is a superb method for drying. My oven has a dehydration cycle that is exceptionally nice. Use the instruction manual that came with your oven.

After your herbs are dry, you can create your own herb seasoning combinations. I keep a small "revolving fines herbes" jar on my counter. Any leftover fresh herbs from dinner preparation are placed on a cake cooling rack until dry. I crumble the dried herbs and place them in the jar. This practice has graphically illustrated for me that there are very few "wrong" combinations of herbs. Experiment with combinations that you think sound good. If you like it, then it is good!

Freezing is one of the most efficient preserving techniques for the home grower and results in the most fresh-like flavor. Place whole leaves or sprigs of herbs on waxed-paper lined cookie sheets. Put cookie sheets in the freezer until the herb leaves are crisp-frozen. Take plastic zip bags to the freezer and working quickly, pour the frozen herbs into the bags. Expel as much air as possible, seal and place inside another zip bag. The frozen herbs will remain flavorful for one season.

Parsley, chives and tarragon can be roughly chopped, frozen as above and kept in small freezer containers. To use the herbs, measure the amount needed and keep the remainder frozen.

Herbs can also be chopped and frozen with a small amount of water or stock in ice cube trays for use in soups and stews.

Dried vs. Fresh. While opinions vary, a rule of thumb is that 1 teaspoon of dried herbs is equal to 1 tablespoon of fresh or frozen. You will learn from experience how much to use in your recipes. Remember also that your dried herbs will lose some of their seasoning strength as they get older. You will want to adjust your seasoning "hand" accordingly.

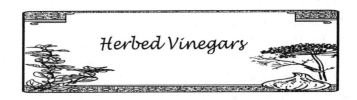

Herbed Vinegars

Herbed Vinegars are truly the crown jewels of the herb garden. Steeping herbs in vinegar is one of the oldest preservation techniques (drying, of course, being the most ancient). What a podium for showcasing your herbs! Herbal vinegars are both beautiful and functional. And, it is the easiest method of all.

Cut fresh herbs in the morning after the dew has dried and the sun has warmed the oils in their leaves. Loosely fill a non-metallic container with the herbs, pour in vinegar to cover the herbs. Cap the container with a non-metallic cap and place in a cool, dark place to steep for three weeks. Vinegars that do not fade in sunlight can be steeped in jugs placed outside on a south-facing porch or deck – just as you would make "sunshine tea." Opal basil, chive and borage should be steeped in the dark to preserve their colors.

The completed vinegar can be used directly from the original container or decanted to fresh, clean bottles and jars. Add a fresh herb sprig and cover. Your vinegars can be bottled in any glass container. Be creative, especially if you wish to give the vinegars as gifts. I have used everything from old Coke and beer bottles to lovely imported Italian blown glass. Antique glass one quart milk bottles are really nice looking.

For a charming gift, cap the bottles with corks. Cut two 7-8" pieces of narrow satin ribbon. Wrap the ribbons around the top of the cork and bottle and dip the bottle tops in melted paraffin. Or, purchase shrink caps from your local home brewing supplier. Make sure you have the right size bottle, however, to accommodate the shrink caps that are available on the market. Make labels on your computer or purchase ready-made labels from novelty stores.

Voila! You now have your own herb garden "crown jewels." And, please don't just let them set on the window sill preening themselves. Use them in salads, fruit salads, stews and sauces. Add a splash to carbonated water for a refreshing drink. Let your imagination be your guide.

One more word about vinegars. Look in specialty food shops for good wine vinegar – both red and white. While cider vinegar is an excellent choice for many of the strong herbs like oregano, wine vinegars provide a softer, warmer base for most recipes. Most food specialty shops can order wine vinegar for you in gallon sizes as well. White distilled vinegar has little virtue as a steeping medium. It is just plain sour.

Now, try your hand at creativity. Use garlic with dill. Add lemon slices and mustard seed to tarragon. Cilantro works with chili peppers. The list is limited only by your willingness to experiment.

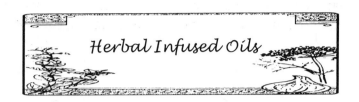

Herbal Infused Oils

Herbal Infused Oils: Today's popular trend of using herb and garlic infused oils needs to be addressed. Unless strict guidelines are observed in the preparation of these oils, there is a real danger of contamination by the bacteria *clostridium botulinum*. According to food and nutrition specialists at Oregon State University, oil that has had raw garlic and herbs added to it should be refrigerated and used in three weeks or less. If using dried herbs and dried garlic, the oil may be safely stored at room temperature for longer periods. Due to their natural acidity, *unseasoned* dried tomatoes may also be stored in oil at room temperature You may add garlic and herbs to the tomatoes *prior* to drying. Dry all ingredients *completely* before placing in oil. Refrigeration is recommended to slow rancidity.

You can flavor olive oil with garlic by heating finely minced raw garlic in a good quality olive oil at a very low temperature (170°) for about 1½ hours. Do not simmer, just gently heat. Remove all traces of the garlic from the oil by straining through several layers of cheesecloth. ALL of the garlic must be removed. Oil flavored in this way is terrific on salads and in stir fry. Again, it is best to refrigerate oils. I make it a point to dispose of all infused oils that are not used within three weeks.

I might also note that the commercial infused oil products found in specialty food stores have been acidified to prevent bacterial growth. Oregon State University researchers do not recommend that we attempt this method at home until more research is conducted.

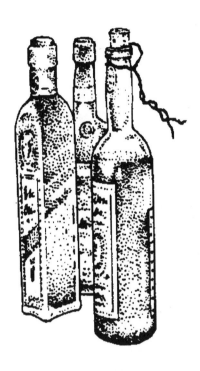

STOCKING
YOUR
SPICE CABINET

Fines Herbes

(feenz airbes)

Fresh or dried, this combination is excellent for seasoning fish, poultry, eggs, and delicate vegetables.

Mix equal portions of dried:

Tarragon   Chervil
Chives   Parsley
Store in a closed jar away from bright
    light and heat.

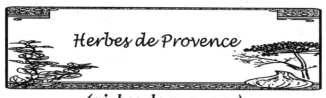

Herbes de Provence

(airbes de pra vonz)

This heady combination of Mediterranean herbs adds its distinctive flavor to lamb, stews, cheese and breads.

Classic Herbes de Provençe:

Equal parts of dried:

Rosemary   Oregano
Savory   Thyme
Lavender   Fennel
Marjoram   Mint

Place in tightly closed jar in dark cool area.

My Favorite Herbes de Provençe Blend:
Equal parts of dried:

Rosemary   Oregano
Savory   Thyme

Bouquet Garni

(boo kay gar nee)

There are several variations of bouquet garni – including your own blend, of course – that make a wonderful complement to stews and soups.

A *Bouquet Garni* is defined as a bundle of herbs and vegetables used for seasoning. The bundle can be fresh herb sprigs tied together or dried herbs placed in a muslin square, bag or tea ball. Coffee filters tied with kitchen string work nicely. The herbs are dropped into a simmering sauce, stew or soup pot. Parsley, thyme and bay leaf are an old standard. The proportion of thyme (or any aromatic herb) depends upon the nature of the dish. A very simple bouquet of parsley leaves can also be used. Rosemary, savory and bay leaf are especially good in lamb dishes. Celery or lovage can be added for the vegetable flavor.

My Favorite Bouquet Garni *(using dried herbs)*:
2 teaspoon parsley flakes
1 teaspoon onion flakes
2 teaspoon celery leaves
½ teaspoon tarragon
½ teaspoon basil
3 peppercorns
1 bay leaf, broken

23

Crumble dried herbs to release some of their flavor. Place all ingredients in bag and add to dish during the last ½ hour of cooking. Check seasoning intensity of your dish after 15 minutes. If you are using the very aromatic herbs, you may wish to remove the bouquet before the cooking time is complete. I make-up a large batch of this mixture and measure 2 Tablespoons, 3 peppercorns and the bay leaf into muslin bags. Store in a tightly-covered tin or jar for future use.

If using fresh herbs, use 2 nice full sprigs of parsley, 2 sprigs of the top 3-4" of celery stalks, one 5" sprig of tarragon, two 3-4" tips of basil sprigs, 1 or 2 bay leaves and 3 peppercorns.

Salad Herb Blend
Sprinkle this mixture on top of salads and soups. Mix 2 Tablespoons with your favorite oil and vinegar combination and allow to steep overnight for an excellent salad dressing.

¼ cup dried parsley
¼ cup dried tarragon
2 teaspoons dried oregano
1 Tablespoon dried dill weed

Place all herbs in food processor. Pulse until herbs are a consistent crumble. Place in tightly covered container and store in a dark place.

Experiment with various herb combinations. Those herbs that you personally prefer in a particular dish are what will set your cooking apart. Make it unique.

Pestos: Ah, the ultimate palate pleaser. Pestos are a bit of work, but worth the effort. Large batches can be made in late summer and stored for winter.

Basil Pesto
This process can be used for many types of pesto, not just the basil variety.

½ cup pine nuts (Coarsely chopped
    black or English walnuts or
    sunflower seeds may also be used.)
3 cloves garlic
4 cups fresh sweet basil leaves
1 cup fresh Italian parsley leaves
¾ cup good quality olive oil
1 cup Coarsely grated Parmesan, Asiago, Romano
    or Pecorino cheese (we prefer Asiago)

Place nuts and garlic in food processor fitted with knife blade. Process to medium chop. Add 2 cups basil leaves and ½ cup parsley leaves. Coarse chop. Add the rest of the basil and parsley. Process to medium chop. With processor running, slowly add olive oil until mixture is thickened enough that it will not run when bowl is tipped. Add cheese and process until mixed. Pesto (like the infused oils discussed earlier) should be refrigerated and used in less than three weeks or frozen in small containers. Float oil on top to keep basil from darkening. Or, fill ice cube trays and freeze. After freezing, remove to zip lock bags. Place bags in second bag as additional protection from freezer burn.

Add ¼ cup pesto to a batch of freshly-cooked pasta. Drop a dollop on top of minestrone soup. Add to salads and dressings.

Mint Pesto
Try this in a Mediterranean salad or cold pasta salad with ripe olives and feta cheese.

¼ cup black walnuts or sunflower seeds
2 cups fresh spearmint leaves
1 cup fresh Italian parsley leaves
3 Tablespoons toasted sesame seeds
¼ cup olive oil
1 teaspoon toasted sesame seed oil
¼ cup Parmesan cheese

Place walnuts or seeds in food processor with knife blade. Process to medium chop. Place spearmint leaves in food processor and process to medium-fine chop. Add parsley and sesame seeds, process to medium-fine chop. With motor running, slowly add oils until mixture is thickened enough that it will not run when bowl is tipped. Add cheese and process until mixed. For a more aromatic pesto, add ¼ cup rosemary leaves.

Oregano Pesto: Substitute 1 cup oregano for the mint and add ¼ cup rosemary leaves – use a little less oil. These blends can be preserved in the same manner as the basil pesto. Since they have a strong flavor you may wish to freeze the pesto in 1 Tablespoon measures in ice cube trays.

BEVERAGES
APPETIZERS
BUTTERS AND
SPREADS

Beverages

Making a perfect cup of herbal tea requires a little practice. Herbal teas do not get as dark as traditional tea so you will need to learn which shade of amber or light green meets your taste preference. Start with fresh cold tap water in your tea kettle. You will also need a tea ball or strainer to keep tea leaves out of your cup, and a china, stoneware or other non-reactive heavy teapot for brewing the tea. Do not use tin or aluminum.

For one cup of herb tea, use 1 teaspoon dried or 3 teaspoons fresh herbs or flowers to one cup of boiling water. For a 6-cup pot, use 2 tablespoons dried or approximately ½ cup fresh herbs to 6-7 cups boiling water. Place herbs in pot. I set my pot on a heavy pot holder to hold the heat. Pour boiling water over herbs. Cover pot or cup with a tea cozy and set timer for 5-8 minutes. At end of brewing time, remove herbs from pot, pour tea and replace the cozy to keep pot hot.

Melissa Root Tea

We developed this tea recipe at our herb farm. Since the botanical name for lemon balm is Melissa officinalis, we named it after my great-grandmother, Melissa Root Luhrs. The addition of lemon balm and spearmint softens the sharp flavor of the peppermint.

½ cup dried, crushed spearmint leaves
¼ cup dried, crushed peppermint leaves
3 Tablespoons dried, crushed lemon balm leaves

Mix herbs together well. Place 3 tablespoons (or to taste) leaves in bottom of stainless or ceramic pot. Pour boiling water over and allow to steep for 8 minutes. Strain into cups. May be sweetened with honey or Lyle's Golden Syrup (available in specialty food stores) if desired.

May Wine

May wine is a May Day tradition in Germany. The flavor of May wine comes from the leaves of the Sweet Woodruff plant (Galium odoratum). Sweet woodruff itself should not be consumed unless it is steeped in an alcoholic beverage such as wine or brandy. The scent of woodruff is reminiscent of vanilla or new-mown hay. A wonderful treat.

1 cup brandy
¼ cup sugar
½ cup fresh sweet woodruff leaves
    (4 Tablespoons dried)
2 750 milliliter bottles of dry white
    wine (Rhine)
1 quart fresh strawberries

Mix the sugar with the brandy. Steep sweet woodruff in the brandy for at least 2 days. To serve, place wine and brandy in a chilled punch bowl. Float strawberries on top. Add some violet flowers for a nice touch.

Easy May Wine

Place several sweet woodruff sprigs in a bottle of white wine. Allow to steep for 3-5 days. Excellent and easy.

Herb Syrups
These syrups are wonderful additions to iced tea,
carbonated water, or fresh cold water

3 cups granulated sugar
2 cups water
1-2 cups roughly chopped
    peppermint or spearmint leaves
    (or a combination of both), OR
    lavender leaves and flowers

Bring sugar and water to boil in a large, heavy saucepan.
Boil for 5 minutes. Remove from heat and mix in herb
leaves. Cover and steep until syrup has cooled. Strain
and place in a covered jar. Store in the refrigerator.

Uses: Place several ice cubes in a large glass. Add 2-4
Tablespoons of syrup. Fill glass with iced tea, carbonated
water or water for a refreshing summer drink. Use as a
topping for ice cream.

Bishop Saint Nicholas Punch

1 Orange
1 Lemon
1 Quart apple cider
2 Tablespoons raisins

½ teaspoon ground cloves
1 Tablespoon brown sugar (optional)
½ teaspoon mace
½ teaspoon nutmeg

Cut orange and lemon in half. Reserve half for slices for garnish in glasses or cups. Squeeze the other half of each into the cider. Add raisins, sugar and spices to cider. Allow to steep overnight. Can serve as is, or strain through cheesecloth for a clearer drink. Serve cold, or hot with cinnamon sticks in mugs.

Herbal Cheesecake

A savory cheesecake with lots of garlic and herbs.
Makes one 9-inch appetizer cake. Can be made as tarts.

1 Tablespoon plus 1/3 cup butter or margarine
1/3 cup unseasoned bread crumbs
¼ cup finely grated Asiago cheese
3 (8 ounce) packages cream cheese, softened
2 cloves garlic, finely chopped
2 Tablespoons dried parsley flakes
1 teaspoon dried oregano leaves
1 teaspoon dried basil
½ teaspoon dried thyme leaves
¼ teaspoon cracked black pepper
1 teaspoon Worcestershire sauce
4 large eggs, at room temperature

Heat oven to 350°. Using 1 tablespoon butter, grease bottom and halfway up side of 9-inch springform pan. In small bowl, combine bread crumbs and grated cheese. Press mixture onto bottom of greased pan. Set pan on baking sheet. Bake 10 minutes. Remove pan to wire rack. Leave oven on.

Melt butter over low heat. In large bowl, with electric mixer at medium speed, beat cream cheese until fluffy. Beat in melted butter, garlic, and herbs until well mixed.

Beat in Worcestershire sauce, then eggs, one at a time. Pour filling over crust in pan.

Bake cheesecake 1 hour. Turn off heat and leave cheesecake in oven 30 minutes with door ajar. Cool on wire rack. Cover cheesecake with plastic wrap and refrigerate.

Marinated Feta Cheese Appetizer

I frequently substitute domestic sheep cheese for the goat cheese in this recipe. Sheep cheese has a milder flavor.

12 ounces goat cheese cut into ¾" cubes
1 cup good olive oil – enough to cover cheese
2 Tablespoons Herbes de Provençe
    (I use equal parts of rosemary, oregano, savory, thyme.
    Lavender, fennel and marjoram can also be added in
    equal parts.)
2 cloves of garlic
8 peppercorns
2 bay leaves
Dried whole red chili peppers to taste

Combine all ingredients and pour over the cheese cubes. Marinate overnight. Serve as hors d'oeuvres on crackers or spooned on top of a salad.

Herbed Cheeses in Seasoned Oil

Due to the addition of garlic to the oil, this mixture should not be stored for more than a few days.

6 ounces cream cheese, softened
8 ounces feta cheese
2 teaspoons finely minced fresh chives
Dried herbs:
1 teaspoon parsley
½ teaspoon savory
½ teaspoon thyme
½ teaspoon marjoram

Process cream cheese and feta cheese in food processor until smooth. Add herbs and process until mixed. Chill for one hour. Place cheese mixture on oiled waxed paper and form into a 2-3" diameter roll. Wrap gently and place on tray in refrigerator until firm. Mix a second batch of dried herbs as above. Process until roughly ground. Sprinkle this batch of herbs on clean waxed paper. Place cheese roll on herbs and roll gently until covered. Chill again for one hour. Reserve leftover rolling herbs. Cut cheese into 1-2" slices and dip cut side in reserved herbs. (Recipe continued on next page.)

Place in a jar with:
2 cups (more or less) good quality olive oil
1 clove garlic (soaked in vinegar overnight and drained)
8 coriander seeds
8 black peppercorns
2 whole allspice
1 sprig each of rosemary, thyme, oregano
1 bay leaf
1 dried hot red pepper

Allow mixture to steep for two days in refrigerator.
Remove cheese slices and serve with crackers on a large
platter. Stunning presentation

Seasoned French Bread
This is so simple. My sons used to fix this in the afternoon after school.

Cut a loaf of French bread in half lengthwise. Spread
each half with a thick coating of mayonnaise. (Light
mayonnaise can be used.) Sprinkle chopped chives,
oregano, chopped onion and Parmesan cheese on each
half. Bake for 15-20 minutes in preheated 350° oven.
Serve warm as an appetizer or with your favorite pasta
meal.

Herb Butters & Spreads

Herb butters are one of the easiest ways to enjoy the vibrant flavors of your herbs. It is a simple matter to add one or several herbs to softened butter. It is not necessary to add the teaspoon of vinegar called for in this recipe. Be creative. Try using summer savory and chive blossoms, rosemary and a touch of balsamic vinegar, basil and some finely grated Romano cheese. Serve herb butter with dinner breads, to make croutons, on French bread. Place a couple pats of herb butter under the skin of chicken or turkey.

Chive Butter

1 cup unsalted butter or butter substitute
1 teaspoon chive flavored vinegar
3 Tablespoons finely minced chives
1 Tablespoon chopped fresh parsley
1 clove garlic, finely minced (Soak garlic clove overnight
   in chive vinegar. Drain before using.)

Cream butter in food processor or mixer, slowly dribble in vinegar while mixer is running. Drain vinegar from garlic. Gently stir in chopped herbs and garlic. Place in container with tight-fitting lid and allow to set overnight before using. Will keep approximately 3 weeks in refrigerator.

37

French Tarragon Butter

1 cup unsalted butter
1 teaspoon tarragon white
   wine vinegar
1-2 Tablespoons fresh chopped
   tarragon
1 teaspoon fresh chopped chervil
½ teaspoon fresh chopped
   spearmint (optional)

Cream butter in food processor or mixer, slowly dribble in vinegar while mixer is running. Gently stir in chopped herbs. Place in container with tight-fitting lid and allow to set overnight before using. Will keep approximately 3 weeks in refrigerator.

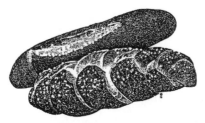

Butter Italia

1 cup unsalted butter, softened
1 clove garlic, soaked overnight in vinegar and drained
1 Tablespoon chopped fresh oregano
1 teaspoon chopped fresh marjoram
1 teaspoon chopped fresh parsley

Mince garlic. Cream butter Gently stir in chopped herbs and garlic. Place in container with tight-fitting lid and allow to set overnight before using. Will keep approximately 3 weeks in refrigerator.

Butter of Provençe
Aïoli

*This olive oil and garlic combination from the Provençe
region is frequently used as a spread, a dip for raw
vegetables and as a sauce for fish and boiled potatoes.*

4 garlic cloves soaked overnight in vinegar and drained
¼ teaspoon salt
2 Tablespoons fine, dry bread crumbs,
    soaked in: 2 teaspoons herbed vinegar
4 egg yolks
1 cup (more or less) good quality olive oil
½ - 1 teaspoon cold water
1 teaspoon lemon juice

Place garlic cloves in food processor and process until
minced. Add the salt and soaked bread crumbs and
process. Add eggs one at a time, processing briefly after
each addition. With processor running, add the olive oil
very slowly until aïoli reaches the consistency you prefer;
then add the water and lemon juice. You may vary any of
the ingredients to achieve the flavor combination that
suits you. Try adding some fresh tarragon or dill for a
different touch. Aïoli may be stored in the refrigerator for
3 days. Whisk slightly if it separates.

39

Herbed Mustard

This is spectacular on a chicken sandwich. It is practically a tradition at our house for leftover turkey sandwiches at Thanksgiving.

2 cups prepared mustard
2 Tablespoons crushed, dried parsley
2 Tablespoons finely crumbled, dried tarragon
1 teaspoon dried dill weed
1½ crushed, dried oregano
2 Tablespoons oregano or tarragon vinegar

Mix mustard and herbs thoroughly. (A food processor can be used.) Stir in vinegar and refrigerate for one week to steep flavors.

Provençal Cheese Spread

2 (8 ounce) packages cream cheese, softened
½ cup unsalted butter, softened
2 cloves garlic, finely minced
1 teaspoon dried oregano
1 teaspoon dried thyme
1 teaspoon dried basil
Freshly ground pepper

Cream the butter and cheese until smooth and fluffy. Add remaining ingredients and mix well. Refrigerate overnight to blend flavors. Bring to room temperature before serving.

Chive Flower Cheese Spread

1 (8 ounce) package cream cheese, softened
1 Tablespoon Chive vinegar (optional)
2-3 Tablespoons fresh, loose chive blossoms
2 Tablespoons Chopped chives
Freshly ground pepper to taste

Cream butter until light and fluffy. Add
vinegar and mix thoroughly. Add chive
blossoms and chives and mix gently.
Refrigerate for several hours before using.

Curry Dip
Especially good as a dip for raw vegetables.

1 cup mayonnaise
½ cup sour cream
2 Tablespoon prepared mustard
½ teaspoon turmeric
½ teaspoon very finely minced garlic
½ teaspoon onion juice (grate onion; use only the juice)
1 teaspoon curry powder

Mix all ingredients gently in a bowl. Refrigerate
overnight to meld flavors.

Basil Cheese Spread

Can also be used as a dip for vegetables.

1 cup rough-chopped basil
½ cup Asiago or Parmesan cheese
¼ cup chopped green onions
2-3 cloves garlic, (Soak in vinegar
   overnight)
¼ cup chopped walnuts
8 ounces cream cheese, softened
½ cup ricotta cheese

Process basil, Asiago cheese, green onions and drained garlic until smooth. Add cream cheese and ricotta cheese and process until smooth. Add walnuts and pulse several times to mix well, but do not overblend. Chill for several hours before serving.

Mocq Boursin

You will receive many compliments from your guests for this ultra-easy version of boursin cheese.

8 ounce package of softened cream cheese
1 clove of garlic, soaked in vinegar overnight, pressed
1 teaspoon each of dried: dill, caraway seed,
   chives and basil
Commercially prepared lemon pepper seasoning

Mix all ingredients except lemon pepper in food processor. Place cheese mixture on a piece of oiled waxed paper. Cover and chill until quite firm. Remove from refrigerator, roll into a 2" diameter log. Place a generous amount of the lemon pepper seasoning on a clean piece of waxed paper. Roll the cheese log in the lemon pepper.

Wrap in plastic wrap and chill thoroughly. Place on a serving platter, slice in 3/8" slices and surround with crackers.

Liver Pâté

1 pound fresh or frozen chicken livers
1 Tablespoon butter
3 Tablespoons mayonnaise
2 Tablespoons lemon juice
2 Tablespoon chopped onion
8 drops bottled hot pepper sauce
1 teaspoon minced rosemary
½ teaspoon salt
½ teaspoon dry mustard
Fresh ground pepper to taste

Cook livers, covered, in the butter until they are no longer pink inside. Place livers and all pan juices in food processor. Add remaining ingredients and blend until very smooth. Adjust seasonings. Place in a crock or ramekin, serve with crackers. May be frozen.

Cucumber Sandwiches

1 medium size cucumber, seeded, grated and drained
1 Tablespoon. mayonnaise
2 teaspoons grated onion
1 teaspoon fresh lemon juice
2 Tablespoons minced fresh parsley
2 Tablespoons minced fresh dill
8 ounces softened cream cheese.

Squeeze out any excess juice from cucumber. Mix remaining ingredients gently and refrigerate. Spread on small bread or bread cutouts and garnish with small piece of unpeeled cucumber and red sweet pepper.

Shrimp Dip
Excellent with crackers or chips.

2 cloves garlic (Soaked in vinegar overnight.)
8 ounces cream cheese
½ cup sour cream
2 Tablespoons capers
1 (5¾ ounce) can of tiny shrimp
1 teaspoon dill weed

Finely chop garlic cloves in food processor. Add cream cheese and process until light and fluffy. Add sour cream and process until mixed. Drain shrimp. Add capers, shrimp and dill weed. Pulse just until mixed. Do not overprocess. Refrigerate overnight.

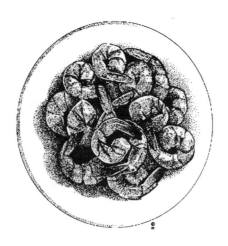

SALADS
DRESSINGS
AND SAUCES

A Salad of Herbs
With Herb Vinaigrette

4 cups whole fresh Italian parsley leaves
2½ cups whole fresh curly parsley leaves
¼ cup fresh mint leaves, coarsely chopped
1 cup small fresh basil leaves
2 Tablespoons fresh tarragon leaves
Toss herbs together well.

Vinaigrette:

5 Tablespoons good quality olive oil
1 Tablespoon tarragon white wine vinegar or
   opal basil white wine vinegar
Salt and pepper to taste

Pour oil into a small bowl, add seasonings and mix well.
Cover and set aside. Just before serving, whisk in the
vinegar until dressing is thickened. Toss with herbs.
Garnish with edible flowers. Serves 8.

Fresh Tomato and Basil Salad
Simple and sure to be a hit with your family.

2 large sun ripened, fresh-from-the-garden tomatoes
12 medium size basil leaves
Olive oil
Salt and fresh ground pepper

Immediately before serving, cut tomatoes into thick slices or quarters. Cut basil leaves julienne style. Alternate layers of tomato, basil , oil, salt and pepper in a serving dish. Splash with some basil vinegar if you wish.

Mediterranean Chicken Salad

2 whole chicken breasts, cooked and cubed
2 cucumbers, seeded and cubed
1½ cup black olives sliced in half
6-8 ounces Feta cheese, cubed
2-3 cloves minced garlic (or, to taste)
2 teaspoons dried dill, or ½ teaspoon dried oregano
½ cup (or, to taste) mayonnaise

Combine all ingredients. Serve on lettuce, croissant or in pita bread.

Raspberry Vinegar Salad Dressing
This makes a wonderful accompaniment to an herbal salad with walnuts.

1 cup walnut oil (or some other light oil)
1 Tablespoon fresh finely chopped basil
1 Tablespoon fresh finely chopped chives
2 teaspoons fresh finely chopped parsley
Salt and fresh ground pepper
¼ cup raspberry vinegar
½ cup toasted walnuts chopped medium coarse

Place oil, herbs and seasonings in a cruet. Shake until well-blended. Or, mix with a fork in a small bowl. Whisk vinegar into mixture until slightly thickened just before serving. Pour over fresh salad greens. Sprinkle coarsely chopped walnuts on top

Roasted Garlic Salad Dressing
A sunny, robust dressing for a green salad.

1 head of roasted garlic (See page 60.)
1/3 cup olive oil
2 tomatoes (about 8 ounces total)
¼ cup chopped green onions
6 Tablespoons fresh basil, finely chopped
2 Tablespoons lemon juice
2 Tablespoons opal basil vinegar

Squeeze pulp from roasted garlic head. Place all ingredients except lemon juice and vinegar in food processor. Process until smooth. Whisk in lemon juice and vinegar immediately before serving.

Balsamic Vinaigrette

1 teaspoon fresh minced thyme
1 Tablespoon fresh minced Italian parsley
1 Tablespoon drained and minced capers
1 clove garlic finely minced
½ teaspoon salt
Fresh ground pepper
5 Tablespoons good olive oil
1½ Tablespoons balsamic vinegar

Mix all ingredients except vinegar with a fork in a small bowl. Whisk vinegar into mixture until slightly thickened just before serving. Pour over fresh salad greens

Citrus Salad Dressing

1 teaspoon finely grated orange rind
½ cup orange juice
2 Tablespoons finely chopped fresh parsley
2 teaspoons finely chopped fresh spearmint
¼ teaspoon Worcestershire sauce
1 teaspoon paprika
½ cup peanut oil
¼ cup rice vinegar

Combine all ingredients except vinegar. Mix well. Whisk vinegar into mixture until slightly thickened just before serving. Pour over fresh salad greens

Chive Sauce
Serve this delicate sauce over asparagus.

3 egg yolks
8 Tablespoons butter
2 Tablespoons fresh chopped chives
1 teaspoon lemon juice
1 teaspoon chive vinegar

Place eggs in top of double-boiler. Whisk over low heat until fluffy. Whisk in butter, one tablespoon at a time. Whisk in lemon juice and then vinegar. Season with a pinch of salt.

Pork Medallion Sage Sauce
Try this with sautéed pork medallions or pork chops.

3 Tablespoons unsalted butter
½ cup finely chopped fresh mushrooms
2 Tablespoons finely chopped green onions
3 Tablespoons flour
½ teaspoon salt
1 Tablespoon finely chopped fresh sage (1 teaspoon dried)
1½ cup chicken broth
½ cup half-and-half

Sauté mushrooms and onion until onion becomes slightly colored. Stir in flour and salt until well blended. Cook for two minutes. Whisk in broth and simmer until thickened. Slowly whisk in sage and half-and-half. Do not boil.

VEGETABLES

Grilled Marinated Vegetables

Marinate any of the following vegetables in the vinaigrette recipe for 2 hours before grilling. (I use a one gallon plastic zip-top bag as a container.) Or, just eat the vegetables fresh as a salad course without grilling.

Zucchini or summer squash, whole or cut into thick slabs
Green onions with 3" of top left on
Small whole yellow onions or 1" slabs of larger onions
Tomatoes, 1" slabs or plum tomatoes halved
Green and/or red sweet peppers cut into 1" thick rings
Baby carrots, whole
Young winter squash 1" thick slices

Vinaigrette:
½ cup raspberry, opal basil or sweet basil vinegar
1 cup olive oil
2 cloves garlic finely minced
¼ cup fresh minced parsley (2 Tablespoons dried)
2 Tablespoons fresh minced sweet basil
   (1 Tablespoon dried)
3 Tablespoons chopped fresh chives
½ teaspoon salt
¼ teaspoon fresh ground black pepper

Place vinegar in bowl of food processor. With machine running and chute open, slowly pour oil in steady stream into chute. Add herbs and seasonings and pulse to mix. Marinate vegetables in mixture for 2 hours.

Remove vegetables from marinade to hot charcoal, gas grill or wood fire. A grill basket makes this task much easier. Most of the vegetables will cook in 3-5 minutes. Tomatoes, 2-3 minutes. Place tomatoes on outer, cooler sections of grill. Winter squash will take 5-7 minutes.

Fresh Marinated Vegetables

Marinade:
2 cups vinegar (sweet basil, opal basil,
    dill or tarragon are excellent)
2 cups olive oil
1-2 Tablespoons of fresh chopped
    basil and parsley
1 Tablespoon fresh
    chopped oregano
2 teaspoons salt if desired
2 Tablespoons sugar
½ teaspoon fresh ground pepper
2 cloves garlic minced
¼ cup instant minced onion (or ½ cup fresh chopped)

Combine ingredients in small saucepan. Bring just to a
boil. Remove from heat and cool thoroughly.

In a large bowl: Combine 4-6 cups fresh vegetables cut
in 1-2" chunks. I use whatever is ready in the garden:
pea pods, tomatoes, zucchini, summer squash, green
pepper, broccoli, cauliflower, baby carrots or carrot slices.

Add:
1 cup fresh coarsely chopped basil
½ cup fresh chopped parsley
2 medium onions thinly sliced

Pour marinade over vegetables and allow to set 4 hours or
overnight in refrigerator.

Rosemary Spinach Bake

10 ounce package of frozen, chopped spinach
1 cup cooked rice
1 cup grated cheddar cheese
2 eggs, beaten
2 Tablespoons butter or margarine softened
1/3 cup milk
2 Tablespoons chopped onion
½ teaspoon Worcestershire sauce
1 teaspoon salt
½ teaspoon fresh chopped rosemary or thyme
   (¼teaspoon dried)

Cook and drain spinach. Mix all ingredients. Pour mixture into 10" x 6" x 1½" casserole dish. Bake at 350° for 20-30 minutes or until knife inserted between center and edge of casserole comes out clean. Cut in squares. Serves 6.

Golden Baked Tomatoes and Zucchini

2 medium zucchini sliced in ¼" thick rounds
3 medium tomatoes cut into 2" chunks
1 large onion sliced ¼" thick
1 green pepper cut into 1" chunks
1 cup fresh grated parmesan
¼ cup fresh, coarsely chopped basil
¼ cup coarsely chopped parsley
1 cup soft bread crumbs
2 Tablespoons olive oil
Salt and pepper

Place a layer of the assorted vegetables 1" deep in the bottom of a casserole. Sprinkle with parmesan cheese, bread crumbs, herbs and salt and pepper and 1-2 teaspoons of olive oil. Repeat layers until all vegetables are used. Top with some parmesan and bread crumbs. Bake 25 minutes at 350° or until vegetables are crisp-tender and top is golden. Serves 4-6.

Basil Zucchini

2 pounds zucchini
½ teaspoon salt
1 Tablespoon butter
1 teaspoon fresh
　chopped basil or
　½ teaspoon dried

Scrub zucchini. Cut into ½" slices. Add salt to ½" boiling water in saucepan. Add zucchini and cover. Cook 5 to 10 minutes until tender. Drain, add butter and basil. Serves 6.

Kale with Marjoram

2½ pounds fresh kale
1 clove garlic, minced
1 teaspoon salt
1 teaspoon fresh finely chopped marjoram
   (½ teaspoon dried)
Freshly ground pepper
½ teaspoon sugar
2 Tablespoons herb vinegar (or cider vinegar)
2 Tablespoons butter or margarine

Wash kale well and discard coarse stems. Place kale, garlic, salt, marjoram, pepper, sugar and 1 Tablespoon vinegar in a large saucepan. Cover and cook 5-8 minutes or until tender. Add remaining vinegar and butter. Heat for 30 seconds. Serves 6.

Tomato Zucchini Sauté

3 medium (8") zucchini
5 plum tomatoes
1 medium onion or 5 green onions with 2" of tops, chopped
1 clove garlic minced
2-3 Tablespoons olive oil
¼ cup fresh chopped chives
2 Tablespoons chopped fresh basil (1 Tablespoon dried)
Salt and fresh ground pepper

Slice zucchini in ½" slices. Remove skins and quarter tomatoes. Heat oil in skillet over medium high heat. Add vegetables and garlic. Sauté 3-4 minutes. Add herbs and continue to cook until crisp-tender. Season to taste.

Stuffed Onions

4 large sweet onions, peeled
1 (10 ounce) package frozen peas
4 ounces fresh sliced mushrooms
½ teaspoon fresh thyme leaves (¼teaspoon dried)
Fresh ground black pepper
1 Tablespoons butter or margarine
¼ cup hot water
½ teaspoon chicken bouillon granules or paste

Slice tops off onions. Hollow out center of each onion
leaving ¼" thick shell. Place onion shells in 8" x 8"
baking dish. Mix peas, mushrooms, thyme and pepper.
Fill each onion with ¼ of the mixture. Dot each onion
with butter. Combine water and chicken stock. Pour over
onions. Cover dish with plastic wrap. Vent one edge.
Microwave on high for 10-15 minutes. Rotate dish
halfway through cooking. Baste with cooking liquid. Let
stand a few minutes before placing in individual serving
dishes. Serves 4.

Fresh Tomato Pasta

This is our family's absolute favorite in the height of summer when tomatoes are at their peak.

5 plum tomatoes (or 3 large regular tomatoes)
1 medium onion
1-2 cloves garlic, pressed or minced
Juice of one lemon
    (or, 2 Tablespoons oregano or basil vinegar)
8 large basil leaves
1 teaspoon fresh rosemary leaves chopped
1 Tablespoon fresh oregano chopped
½ cup olive oil
Salt and fresh ground pepper
Grated Italian cheese (Asiago, Parmesan or Romano)

Combine all ingredients two hours before serving. Prepare one pound of pasta (more or less, depending upon how much sauce you like in proportion to pasta). Drain pasta and pour sauce over hot pasta. Sprinkle with grated cheese.

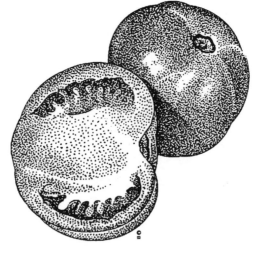

58

Minted Baby Carrots

1½ pounds baby carrots
2 Tablespoon corn oil
2 teaspoons finely chopped fresh ginger
2 Tablespoons minced green onion with tops
3 Tablespoons honey
2 Tablespoons tamari sauce
1 Tablespoon lemon juice
¼ cup orange juice
2 Tablespoons finely chopped fresh spearmint
Salt and pepper to taste

Steam the carrots until crisp-tender. Drain carrots and sauté for two minutes in the corn oil. Add ginger and green onions. Sauté until onion is soft. Mix honey, tamari sauce, lemon juice and orange juice. Add to carrots and simmer very slowly until carrots are tender and glazed (about 5-8 minutes). Add salt and pepper and the chopped mint. Simmer for two minutes.

Sautéed Swiss Chard

3 pieces of thick sliced bacon
1 Tablespoon finely chopped green onion
1 pound Swiss chard
1 Tablespoon unsalted butter (optional)
Salt and pepper

Wash, drain and trim tough stems from Swiss chard. Cut into strips. Fry bacon until crisp. Drain and crumble. Remove all but 2 Tablespoons drippings from pan. Add onion and sauté until soft. Add the Swiss chard and butter (optional). Simmer until chard is soft. Toss bacon and seasonings with chard. Serve immediately.

Roasted Garlic

Roasting garlic brings out a soft, nutty flavor in the garlic. It can be used as an appetizer spread on bread or crackers, added to soups, blended into deglazing liquid for a sauce, rubbed on a roasting chicken or added to your favorite pasta sauce. I use a terra-cotta roaster, but aluminum foil or any heavy, oven-proof casserole dish will work.

4 whole, fresh, firm garlic heads (or more as needed)
1-2 Tablespoons olive oil

- Remove any loose papery skins from garlic heads but do not strip all of the skin away.
- With a sharp knife, cut the top ½" of garlic head away, exposing the tips of the cloves.
- *For a milder flavor, garlic may be poached for 10 minutes in 1 cup of milk and rinsed prior to roasting.*
- **Covered Casserole Dish:** Place garlic heads in casserole dish just large enough to hold them. Drizzle with olive oil. Cover dish. Place in preheated 350° oven for approximately 45 minutes.
- **Aluminum foil:** Place each prepared garlic head on an 8 – 10" piece of heavy duty foil. Drizzle with olive oil. Pull foil up around the garlic head. Twist to close. Place on a tray in 350° oven for 45 minutes.
- **Terra-cotta roaster:** Do not preheat oven. Soak the top of the roaster for 15 minutes before placing in oven. Roast for an hour.
- **To serve:** Separate the cloves. Using your fingers or the back of a butter knife, squeeze out the pulp. Store unused portions in a tightly covered container in refrigerator for 4 or 5 days.

Roasted Red Sweet Peppers

I have always avoided dishes that call for roasted peppers because of the work involved. This method for roasting/charring peppers is very easy. The results are magnificent for use in salads and pasta sauces.

3 large red sweet peppers

- Preheat broiler to 500°.
- Slice ¼" to ½" off both ends of the peppers. Remove the stem from the top slice.
- Remove core from pepper and slit the pepper down one side so that you have one long strip of pepper. Remove all membranes and seeds in pepper. Place pepper strips skin-side up on a foil-lined cookie sheet. Flatten peppers as much as possible with your hands.
- Roast 2-3 " from broiler until skin is puffy and charred. Watch closely. It will only take a few minutes. Turn pan after 5 minutes to evenly char peppers. Broil for another 5 minutes.
- Remove from oven, cool slightly and carefully peel the skin. If you wish, peppers can be removed to a bowl and covered with plastic wrap to steam them briefly to more easily remove skins.
- Peppers can be cut into strips or pureed for various recipes. They may be stored for a day or two before losing some of their vitality.

Roasted Garlic and Sweet Pepper Tomato Sauce

This is so good! Roasted garlic and peppers add a mellow flavor to this outstanding sauce. Serve over pasta or use as a dip for bread sticks.

2 pounds plum (Italian) tomatoes
The pulp from 4 heads of roasted garlic
2 large red sweet peppers, roasted and coarsely chopped
1 (28 ounce) can of Italian style whole tomatoes
1 (28 ounce) can of Italian style crushed tomatoes
1 Tablespoon each of chopped fresh rosemary,
    basil and oregano
3 cloves garlic, chopped
¼ cup olive oil
Salt and pepper

Cut tomatoes into quarters and remove most of the seeds. Place in large, shallow, non-aluminum roasting pan. Add roasted garlic pulp, roasted sweet peppers, the whole canned tomatoes cut into quarters and seeded, herbs and fresh garlic and approximately ½ of the can of crushed tomatoes. Reserve the balance to thin the sauce if needed. Place in pre-heated, 325° oven for 30-45 minutes until thickened. Remove from oven and cool. Put the sauce in food processor in batches and puree. Season. Serve hot over angel hair pasta with a grating of parmesan cheese.

BREADS
AND
PASTAS

BREADS

Herbes de Provençe Sourdough Bread

1 cup sourdough starter
1 1/3 cups warm water
5-6 cups all-purpose flour
1 Tablespoon salt
1 Tablespoon sugar
1 teaspoon baking soda
2-3 Tablespoons each of minced oregano,
   thyme and rosemary
Cornmeal to sprinkle on pans

- Pour 1 cup of starter into a large ceramic bowl.
- Add the warm water and 3 cups of flour. Beat vigorously.
- Cover with plastic wrap and put aside to rise for 4 to 24 hours. (The longer period is preferable.)
- After the sponge has bubbled and expanded, blend the salt, sugar and baking soda into 2 cups of flour.
- Add the finely chopped herbs to the sponge and mix well.
- Add the flour mixture and mix until the dough begins to hold together.
- Turn dough out onto a floured board and knead for 3-4 minutes. Add flour as needed to make a fairly stiff dough. Allow the dough to rest while you clean and grease the mixing bowl. Continue to knead dough for another 4 minutes.

- Place dough in the prepared bowl, turning to grease the top. Cover with a dampened dish towel and allow to rise for 2 to 4 hours.
- Gently press the dough down and shape into one large or two French style loaves. Place on a cornmeal sprinkled cookie sheet or baking stone and let rise for another 2 hours. Loaves will look a little flat. They will rise in the oven.
- Toward the end of the rising period, preheat the oven to 450°. Slash the tops of the loaves diagonally about ¼" deep every two inches. Bake for 25 minutes or until they sound hollow when tapped.
- This dough can also be made into a braid for an outstanding presentation at the table.

Savory Herb Bread

2½ - 3 cups unbleached flour
2 packages rapid rise yeast
2 Tablespoons sugar
1 teaspoon salt
1½ teaspoons each: fresh chopped
    chives, thyme and parsley (or,
    marjoram, oregano and thyme)
½ cup milk
½ cup water
4 Tablespoons butter
1 egg
1 cup whole wheat flour
2 more teaspoons of the fresh chopped herb combination

Combine 1½ cups flour, dry yeast, sugar, salt, and 4½ teaspoons herbs in a large bowl. Heat milk, water and 3 Tablespoons butter to 125°-130°; stir into yeast mix. Add egg, whole wheat flour and enough remaining flour to make a soft dough. Knead on lightly floured board for 4 minutes. Let dough rest for 10 minutes and knead for 4 more minutes.

On lightly floured surface, divide dough into three equal pieces. Roll each to 14-inch rope. Braid ropes; pinch ends to seal. Place in greased 8½" x 4½" bread pan. Cover; let rise until doubled. Bake in preheated 375° oven for 25 to 30 minutes or until golden. Melt remaining 1 Tablespoon butter; brush on loaf, sprinkle with reserved 2 teaspoons herbs. Remove from pan, cool on wire rack.

Basil Pesto Bread Variation: Make bread as above, but eliminate herbs. Allow dough to rise until double. Roll dough into a 10" x 12" rectangle. Spread a thin layer of pesto on dough, leaving 1" margins all around. Starting on the 12" side, roll into a log. Seal edges and place sealed side down in bread pan. Allow to rise for a few minutes. Bake in preheated 375° oven for 25-30 minutes or until golden and hollow sounding when tapped. Remove to cooling rack. Best served warm.

Flowerpot Herbed Bread

These little pots of bread are always a hit at our luncheon and afternoon tea parties

You will need at least 8 NEW small (3 ½") clay flower pots. Wash pots in warm water with a very small amount of detergent and rinse well. Dry thoroughly and brush the inside of pots with vegetable oil. Place them in the oven on a cookie sheet and heat oven to 450°. Bake for one hour. Cool pots. Cut parchment paper circles to fit in bottom of pots.

Make your favorite 5-6 cup-of-flour bread recipe. Knead 1 or 2 Tablespoons of herbs of your choice into dough. (Rosemary, dill, basil or chives are very good.) Allow bread to rise as usual. Punch bread down and pinch off 2" rounds of bread. Form into a ball. Roll balls in melted butter to which you have added some finely-chopped herbs. Place 3 dough balls in each flowerpot. Allow to rise for ½ hour and bake in 350° oven for 10-15 minutes or until golden brown. Place one flowerpot at each guest's place.

Focaccia

An Italian flat bread topped with coarse salt, olive oil and other seasonings of choice

1 Tablespoon dry yeast
1 ½ cups warm water
4 - 5 cups all-purpose flour
2 teaspoons salt
2 Tablespoons olive oil

- Dissolve the yeast in the water for 15 minutes.
- Mix 4 cups of flour with the salt in a large bowl. Make a well in the center of the flour.
- Pour the yeast mixture and the olive oil into the well.
- Mix flour from outside edges and continue mixing until dough forms a ball.
- Knead by hand with additional flour to make a soft dough (about 6 minutes). Cover and set aside until double.
- **Toppings:** Use any, or several of the following toppings: Thinly sliced tomatoes, sun-dried tomatoes, thinly sliced onions that have been soaked in salted water, rinsed and patted dry, feta cheese, chopped garlic, basil, oregano, or rosemary, about 1 Tablespoon coarse salt and ¼ cup olive oil. (Or, any of your own creations.)
- Preheat the oven (and baking stone or tiles if you use them) to 400° for 30 minutes before baking.
- When the dough has finished rising, remove to counter. Roll the dough into a 10 inch square, or two smaller circles.
- Place dough on a baking sheet, or on an oven peel sprinkled with semolina flour.

- Place toppings and herbs on dough, pushing them into the dough lightly. Drizzle with olive oil. (I make little indentations with my thumb before drizzling the olive oil over the dough.) Lightly sprinkle the coarse salt over all.
- Set the dough aside to rise for 15-20 minutes before sliding into the oven and baking for 30 minutes.
- Remove to wire rack and eat while warm.

Hot Dilled Corn Muffins

1 cup flour
1¼ cup yellow cornmeal
1 Tablespoon baking powder
1 Tablespoon sugar
¾ teaspoon salt
½ teaspoon flaked, dried cayenne pepper
2 teaspoons dried dill weed
1 egg
3 Tablespoons melted butter
1 cup milk

Grease corn bread pan, muffin pan or 9" x 9" heavy square pan well. Place in preheated 425° oven while mixing muffins. Combine all dry ingredients, mix well. Place egg, butter and milk in a **2 cup** measuring cup. Beat well with a hand egg beater. Combine quickly with dry ingredients, mixing just until moistened. Carefully remove preheated pan from oven. Place batter in pan and bake corn sticks for approximately 15 minutes; cake pan or muffins for 20-25 minutes. Serve with butter.

Herb Waffles

An excellent brunch item. The onion adds a special touch.
Top with herb butter and serve with sausage.

2 cups flour
1 Tablespoon baking powder
½ teaspoon salt
1¾ cup milk
2 large eggs
1/3 cup melted butter
1 Tablespoon finely chopped
   fresh parsley
1 Tablespoon grated onion
1 teaspoon finely ground fresh sage (½ teaspoon dried)
1 teaspoon finely minced fresh thyme (½ teaspoon dried)

Heat waffle iron. Combine flour, baking powder and salt.
Beat the milk into the eggs. Add the herbs and onion to
the butter, add to the milk mixture and mix well. Pour
into the dry ingredients and stir until just blended. Pour
batter on hot waffle iron and spread batter to the edges of
iron. Bake until steam stops rising. Serves 4.

Basic Pasta Dough

Making your own pasta is not only satisfying, it allows you to add herbs to your product. If you have 45 minutes in which to prepare dinner, you can make your own pasta.

¾ cup unbleached bread flour
¼ cup semolina flour
1 teaspoon olive oil
1 egg
Water to moisten
10 -15 medium-sized, clean, fresh,
   dry basil leaves

- Place unbleached flour and semolina in food processor bowl fitted with dough blade.
- Pulse to mix.
- Sprinkle in oil and add egg. Mix until evenly granulated.
- With machine running, dribble water in, 1 teaspoon at a time – just until dough starts to hold together.
- Process for 20 seconds to knead dough.
- Remove from processor and knead by hand 8-10 times. Do not use flour on board unless dough sticks.
- Cover with a damp cloth and set aside for 15 minutes.
- Divide into 4 portions. Flatten one portion into a rectangle. Keep remaining portions covered.
- If dough is sticky, dust lightly with flour.

71

- Place pasta machine dial on #1. Run dough through machine. If dough is too dry, dampen with water.
- Fold dough in half and run through machine again. Continue to do this until dough feels smooth, elastic and velvety – 4 or 5 times.
- Turn dial to #2. Run dough through once, do not fold.
- Continue in this manner through #5 on the dial. Lay fresh towel-dried basil leaves from the middle to the end of the long strips.
- Fold dough over to cover basil leaves. Press edges firmly closed.
- Run each strip through dial #5 and #6.
- Lay strips on cake cooling rack. Cover with a dry towel.
- When all of the sections of dough have been rolled out, cut strips by running dough through angel hair attachment (or, attachment of your choice). Gently guide dough over roller.
- When all of the strips are cut, drop into boiling, salted water. Cook rapidly for 4-8 minutes until al denté. Check frequently as cooking time will vary depending on moisture content of pasta.
- You can freeze any pasta that you do not cook. This recipe yields approximately ¾ pound dry pasta.

Cheese and Garlic Pasta

4 Tablespoons butter, or olive oil
2 cloves of garlic, pressed
Asiago, parmesan or romano cheese

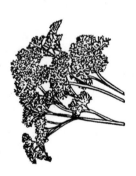

Boil ¾ pound of pasta. Melt or heat
butter or oil in microwave. Add
pressed garlic and microwave another 10 seconds. Heat a
large pasta bowl by filling it with hot tap water. When
pasta is nearly done, empty bowl and towel it dry.
Remove pasta from water with spaghetti tongs directly to
preheated bowl. Toss pasta with garlic mixture. Sprinkle
with cheese and fresh ground black pepper.

Fresh Herbs and Pasta

¼ cup unsalted butter
1 Tablespoon dijon or
    stone-ground mustard
2 Tablespoons olive oil
¼ cup fresh chopped flat-leaf
parsley
1½ Tablespoons fresh chopped
tarragon
¼ cup fresh chopped basil leaves
1 Tablespoon chopped dill weed
2 Tablespoons chopped chives
1 pound angel hair pasta
Salt and fresh ground black pepper

Mix melted butter with mustard and olive oil. Cook pasta
in salted water just until tender. Place in warmed
serving bowl and toss with the mustard mixture and
herbs. Season to taste and serve immediately.

73

Bowtie Pasta with Fresh Salmon

¼ cup olive oil
1 teaspoon minced garlic
¼ teaspoon red pepper flakes
2 cups canned whole peeled
    Italian tomatoes with juice,
    coarsely chopped
Salt
8 ounces bowtie pasta
½ pound fresh, cooked, boned salmon cut in ½" chunks
1 cup heavy cream
2 Tablespoons shredded fresh basil

Sauté garlic and peppers in olive oil until garlic turns
light golden. Add tomatoes and salt. Simmer on medium-
low heat for 20 minutes or until sauce separates from the
oil. Remove from heat and set aside.

Bring 4 quarts of water to boil, add 1 Tablespoon of salt
and drop-in pasta. Return skillet to medium high heat,
add the cream and a pinch of salt to the tomato mixture.
Cook until the cream is reduced by one-half. Add basil
and salmon chunks. Heat just until salmon and basil are
warmed and remove from heat. Toss cooked pasta with
the sauce and serve immediately.

SOUPS
MAIN DISHES
MEAT & FISH

Soups

Chicken Wing Soup

1 pound chicken wings
2 cups water
1 cup tomato juice
2 teaspoons salt
6 peppercorns
¼ cup margarine or butter
1 cup chopped celery
1 cup chopped onion
2 Tablespoons flour
Broth from cooked wings
1 cup milk or half-and-half
2 teaspoons dried dill weed
½ teaspoon dried
   thyme leaves

Cook wings in water, juice, salt and peppercorns for 20-30 minutes. Strain broth and reserve broth and chicken. Remove meat from bones and dice. Sauté onions and celery in margarine until onion is translucent, but not brown. Stir in flour, reserved broth, milk, chicken and herbs. Bring to a simmer, stirring constantly until slightly thickened. Serve with a dollop of sour cream or yogurt, garnished with fresh dill.

Santa Fe Cheese Soup

Cut 2 large, peeled carrots; 1 small, peeled onion and
    1 small, cored apple into 1-inch pieces
3 small jalapeño or serrano chilies, seeded

3 Tablespoons unsalted butter
2 cups chicken stock
½ cup dry white wine
6 Tablespoons unbleached all purpose flour
2 cups milk
6 ounces cheddar cheese
6 ounces chilled Monterey Jack cheese
Salt and freshly ground pepper
½ cup fresh cilantro, minced
2 small plum tomatoes, seeded and diced

- In food processor, process carrots, onion, apple and peppers until finely minced.
- Melt butter in large saucepan over medium-low heat.
- Add contents of food processor and cook until softened, stirring occasionally, about 8 minutes.
- Add stock and wine and bring to boil. Reduce heat, cover and simmer gently until vegetables are very soft, about 30 minutes.
- Puree vegetable mixture in food processor until very smooth.
- Press through fine strainer into bowl.

- Place flour in another large bowl. Gradually whisk in half of milk, making smooth paste.
- Mix in strained vegetable mixture and remaining milk.
- Return to sauce pan. Cook over medium heat until slightly thickened, stirring constantly, about 2 minutes.
- Shred cheddar and Monterey Jack cheeses. Stir cheeses into soup.
- Cook over medium heat until smooth, stirring frequently. Season with salt and pepper. (Can be prepared 3 days ahead.)
- Mix cilantro and tomatoes. Ladle soup into bowls; spoon a dollop of tomato mixture into center of each bowl. Makes about 5 cups.

Cream of Brie and Leek Soup
Use a good quality brie.

½ cup unsalted butter
6 large leeks (white parts only)
　　finely chopped
4 cups unsalted chicken stock
½ cup flour
4 cups half and half
1 ½ pounds Brie cheese with rind on,
　　chilled, cut into small cubes
2 Tablespoons chopped fresh chives
2 Tablespoons chopped fresh Italian parsley
Pepper

Melt ¼ cup of the butter in a large deep pan over medium heat. Add leeks and cook until translucent, stirring frequently. Add chicken stock, cover and simmer until leeks are tender. Puree in blender or food processor. Melt remaining butter in heavy non-aluminum saucepan over medium heat. Add flour and cook for 2 minutes, stirring constantly. Blend in half and half 1 cup at a time. Whisk until smooth. Add ¼ of cheese at a time and blend until smooth. Strain. Return to pan and add leek puree. (Can be prepared several hours ahead and reheated.) Thin with more chicken stock if needed. This soup is very rich. Serve in ½ cup servings sprinkled with pepper and chopped chives.

Chilled Tomato Soup

4 medium large tomatoes (about 1 pound)
1 tablespoon chopped green onion with tops
2 teaspoons fresh lime juice
4 ice cubes
½ teaspoon salt
Fresh ground pepper to taste
2 teaspoons chopped fresh dill weed
1 tablespoon plain yogurt or sour
  cream thinned with 1 teaspoon milk

Place peeled and quartered tomatoes,
onion, lime juice, ice cubes, salt and pepper in food
processor or blender. Blend until smooth. Force through
a sieve, pressing hard to get all liquid. Stir in dill. Place
in bowls with a dollop of yogurt or sour cream. Garnish
with fresh dill sprig. Serve immediately.

Savory Pâte à Choux
(Herbed cheese cream puff)
*This twist on the traditional cream puff makes superb fare
for an herbal luncheon.*

1 cup water
1/3 cup butter
1 cup flour
¼ teaspoon salt
4 or 5 eggs
   (*at room temperature*)
1 cup grated cheese (Swiss,
   cheddar, or Edam)
1 Tablespoon fresh chopped dill weed
1 Tablespoon fresh chopped chive tops

Preheat oven to 400°. Place water and butter in heavy
pan. Bring to boil, remove from heat and add flour and
salt all at once. Stir quickly to incorporate flour. Return
to heat and stir rapidly until dough does not cling to the
sides of pan. Remove from heat and incorporate eggs one
at a time, beating after each egg. Continue to beat until
the dough no longer looks wet. Stir in 2/3 cup cheese and
herbs. Drop by tablespoon on parchment covered cookie
sheet. Top with remaining cheese. Bake for 10 minutes
and reduce the heat to 350° and bake 15 to 20 minutes
longer until golden. Best served warm.

81

Fresh Mozzarella Pizza

Made with the same dough as the focaccia recipe, topped with 'fresh' tomato sauce and fresh mozarella.

One recipe of focaccia dough. (See page 68.) Allow dough to rise until double. Preheat oven (with baking stone or tiles in place) for 30 minutes to 500°.

Topping:
2 or 3 garlic cloves, minced
3 cups canned crushed tomatoes with thick sauce,
    coarsely chopped. (The Italian tomatoes in food
    specialty shops are especially good for this recipe.)
Fresh mozarella cheese sliced (if available – otherwise
    use packaged variety)
2 Tablespoons coarsely chopped basil and rosemary
    (or your choice of herbs)
Olive oil, salt and pepper

Sauté garlic in olive oil over medium heat for 30 seconds. Add tomatoes. Simmer until sauce is slightly thickened and not watery. Season with salt and pepper.

Turn dough onto lightly floured surface and cut into halves or quarters, depending upon the diameter and thickness you prefer. Carefully stretch the dough into the size you want. Sprinkle semolina flour on an oven peel and lay dough on the peel. Brush a light coating of olive oil on the dough add toppings and sprinkle chopped herbs on top. DO NOT add cheese until last two minutes of baking period. Carefully slide onto baking stone. Bake, checking frequently , until crust turns light golden.

Polish Spaghetti

This recipe has been handed down from my mother's family. It has as its origin, the Polish-Italian neighborhood that my grandparents lived in upon immigrating to America. Its flavor is unique. The recipe is large and freezes well.

3½ pounds lean ground round
2 of the long links of smoked Polish sausage
1 large green pepper
3 medium onions
3 ounce jar of green olive pieces
5 cups tomato sauce
2-3 cloves garlic pressed
2 Tablespoons chopped fresh oregano
   OR 2 teaspoon dried
1-2 cups fresh sliced mushrooms
Fresh ground pepper to taste
Salt should not be needed

Grind polish sausage on coarse blade of meat grinder and brown with ground round in a non-stick pan or in as little oil as possible. Grind green pepper, onions and olives with coarse blade of meat grinder. (Or, use food processor with knife blade to a medium chop. Do not over process.) Drain any grease from the meat. Place browned meat, green pepper, onion, and olives in large non-aluminum pan. Add tomato sauce and garlic. Simmer for approximately 2 hours until mixture thickens. If it becomes too thick, add more tomato sauce. Add oregano, mushrooms and pepper. Cook another 15-20 minutes. Serve over spaghetti with grated cheese. Any extra fat from the sausage should be skimmed before serving.

Quiche Lorraine
Simple and elegant, quiche can be a meal in itself.

Pastry for 10" (1" deep) quiche pan:
1¼ cups sifted all-purpose flour
¼ teaspoon salt
2 Tablespoons shortening
4 Tablespoons cold butter
3-4 Tablespoons cold water

Sift flour and salt into bowl. Add the shortening and blend with pastry blender. Cut the butter into small pieces and blend until mixture looks like coarse meal. Sprinkle 3 Tablespoons cold water over mixture and mix gently with a fork. Lightly form into a ball, adding more water if necessary. Flatten the dough ball slightly, place between layers of waxed paper and chill for 30 minutes. Leaving dough between waxed paper sheets, roll out to approximately a 13-14" circle. Place the dough in the quiche pan and trim excess dough to top of pan. Chill for 30 minutes. Preheat oven to 400°. Line the pan with aluminum foil and cover bottom of foil with a layer of pie weights or beans. Bake for 10 minutes. Remove foil and beans. (I save the beans to be used again for this purpose.) Prick the bottom and sides of the crust every 2" inches or so with a fork and return to 375° oven for 10 more minutes or until lightly tanned. Remove shell from oven. Leave oven on.

Filling:

¼ pound bacon crisp-fried and crumbled
2 Tablespoons finely chopped green onion with 3" of tops.
1 cup grated Swiss or Gruyère cheese (or a combination)
3 eggs
1 Tablespoon flour
1 cup half-and-half (milk can be substituted,
   but can result in a watery filling)
2 teaspoons fresh finely minced tarragon (1 t. dried)
Fresh ground black pepper
1 Tablespoon melted butter

Place bacon, onion and cheese in baked pastry. In a separate bowl, whisk the flour into the eggs. Mixture doesn't have to be smooth. Mix in the remaining ingredients. Place quiche pan on oven rack. Pour the egg mixture into pan and carefully slide shelf in and close oven. Bake for 30 minutes until golden and puffed. Insert knife between center and edge of pan. If knife comes out clean, remove quiche from oven. Cool slightly and serve warm or cold with a fresh garden salad.

Omelette Casserole

16 slices of bread with crusts removed
¾ pound grated cheddar cheese
1-2 cups cooked ham, crab or shrimp pieces
6 eggs
3 cups milk
½ teaspoon dry mustard
½ teaspoon dried oregano
½ teaspoon dried dill weed
Salt and pepper to taste
1 cup crushed corn flakes
¼ cup melted butter

Butter large shallow pan. Butter bread lightly. Place
half of the bread slices in bottom of pan. Top with cheese
and meat chunks. Place other half of bread on top. Beat
eggs, milk and seasonings together and pour over the
other ingredients. **Refrigerate overnight.** Sprinkle
corn flakes and butter over top of casserole. Cover with
foil and bake for 45 minutes at 350°. Remove foil and
bake 5-10 minutes more until lightly browned. Garnish
with sprigs of young, fresh dill. Serves approximately 8.

Welsh Rarebit with Smoked Turkey Breast

This is a special taste treat. My family never cared for this dish until I started using the smoked turkey.

4 individual pieces of broccoli with stem
½ cup beer
8 ounces sharp Cheddar, grated
1 egg, slightly beaten
1 teaspoon Worcestershire sauce
2 teaspoons finely chopped fresh tarragon
Salt to taste
Fresh ground pepper
½ teaspoon dry mustard
4 slices of smoked turkey breast
4 slices of bread, or, 2 Kaiser onion rolls cut in half

Steam the broccoli pieces until tender. Place beer in top of double boiler over hot water. When the beer is warm, gradually stir the cheese in until melted. Stirring constantly, stir in the egg. Add seasonings. Toast bread or rolls. Place a warmed piece of turkey and a stem of broccoli on each piece of bread. Pour cheese mixture over each serving. Garnish with a small tarragon sprig.

Meat & Fish

Holiday Roast Beef

Marinade:
2 cups Burgundy
2 medium onions, finely chopped
2 cloves garlic, quartered
3 bay leaves
1 teaspoon dried thyme leaves
6 pound sirloin-tip beef roast
1 cup finely diced carrot
1 cup chopped celery
6 parsley sprigs
12 black peppercorns
3 Tablespoons flour
¾ cup beef broth
¼ cup Burgundy
¼ teaspoon salt

Prepare the marinade the day before cooking the roast. Pour 2 cups of Burgundy into a large bowl. Add onion, garlic, bay leaves and thyme. Wipe roast and place in bowl. Turn and prick with a fork several times. Cover bowl and refrigerate overnight. Preheat oven to 325°. Place meat in shallow, open roasting pan. Insert thermometer into thickest part of roast. Save marinade. Roast uncovered about 3 hours at 325°, or to internal temperature of 140° for rare, or 160° for medium. One-half hour before roast is done, combine carrot, celery, parsley and peppers with marinade and pour over roast.

Remove finished roast to platter. Strain vegetables from drippings. Reserve broth and vegetables. Return 3 Tablespoons fat to pan. Add flour to fat and stir until smooth. Add water to drippings to make 1 ½ cups and gradually add this with the beef broth and Burgundy to the flour mixture. Stir until smooth. Simmer gently until thickened.

Beef Stew

2 pounds beef chuck roast cut into 1½" cubes
1 teaspoon salt
½ teaspoon ground pepper
2-4 Tablespoons oil
1 medium onion chopped
1 clove garlic minced
3 Tablespoons flour
1 Tablespoon lemon juice
1 Tablespoon Worcestershire
1 full teaspoon beef bouillon paste (I use Minor's brand)
1 cup Burgundy
2 cups hot water
1 teaspoon thyme dried
1 bay leaf
6 medium carrots cut into 1" chunks
6 medium potatoes cubed
2 Tablespoons fresh chopped parsley

Preheat oven to 225°. Place meat in a large bowl. Sprinkle with salt and pepper and mix well. Heat oil in heavy non-aluminum pan. Brown meat over medium-high heat. Remove meat from pan. Add onion and cook for 4 minutes. Reduce heat to medium; add garlic and cook for 1 minute, stirring constantly. Add flour and cook for 2 minutes, stirring constantly. Stir in lemon juice, Worcestershire sauce and beef bouillon. Stir until well blended. Add wine and stir until all browned bits have been scraped from bottom of pan. Return meat to pan, add thyme, bay leaf and 2 cups of water. Bring to a simmer, cover and place in oven. Cook for 1 hour. Add carrots and potatoes and cook for another 1½-2 hours until meat is tender. Stir in parsley, remove bay leaf and serve. Serves 4.

Meat Loaf

1 cup catsup
2 Tablespoons brown sugar
2 Tablespoons vinegar (basil flavored is good)
¼ cup water
1 cup small, dry bread cubes
½ cup chopped green pepper
½ cup chopped onion
1 teaspoon dried oregano or marjoram
½ teaspoon salt
1 clove of garlic, pressed
1 egg
1½ pounds ground chuck (or mixture of pork, veal & beef)

In a large bowl, mix catsup, sugar and vinegar. Reserve ½ cup for topping. Add water, bread cubes, green pepper, onion, oregano, salt, garlic and egg. Allow to stand for 5 minutes. Add ground meat; mix well and pack into a greased loaf pan. Top with reserved sauce. Bake at 350° for 50 minutes or until done. Allow to stand for 15 minutes before serving.

Herbed Pork Roast

3 pound boneless pork loin roast
2 cloves garlic – each clove sliced
    into 3 pieces
1/3 cup Dijon style mustard
1 teaspoon dried thyme crushed
½ teaspoon dried rubbed sage
Salt and fresh ground pepper
8 baby onions
½ cup good white wine

Preheat oven to 425°. Make small slits in the roast and
insert garlic slices. Mix mustard, thyme, sage, salt and
pepper in a small bowl. Rub mixture over the outside of
roast. Place roast in shallow roasting pan, arrange peeled
onions around roast and add wine. Place roast in oven
and immediately turn heat down to 325°. Using a meat
thermometer, roast pork to 170°. Remove roast and
onions to a warmed serving platter. Reserve drippings for
sauce or gravy. Serves 4-6 people.

Rosemary Roasted Lamb

We traditionally have lamb for dinner on Christmas Day. This recipe has become one of our favorites. Balsamic vinegar adds a note of warmth and sweetness to the marinade.

1 (4 to 5 pound) lamb rolled shoulder roast
2 cups olive oil
2 cups balsamic vinegar
4 Tablespoons fresh minced rosemary leaves (2 T. dried)
4-6 cloves garlic
1 teaspoon fresh ground pepper
Salt to taste

Thinly slice 2 cloves of garlic. Slip slivers of garlic into the folds of the rolled roast. Mince remaining garlic and place in bowl of food processor with vinegar, rosemary and pepper. With machine running, add olive oil in steady stream through food chute. Place lamb in large food-safe plastic bag or non-reactive bowl. Marinate overnight. Preheat oven to 450°. Remove lamb from marinade, sprinkle lightly with salt and place on a rack in a lightly-oiled, shallow roasting pan in oven. Lower oven temperature to 325° and roast for approximately 30 minutes per pound. Gravy can be made with the drippings.

Tarragon Chicken Bake

This is marvelously easy. Our sons fixed it while in college and impressed their roommates no end.

3 pound frying chicken cut into pieces or 4 whole breasts
2 Tablespoons tarragon vinegar
1 Tablespoon fresh tarragon leaves slightly
   chopped (2 teaspoons dried)
2 Tablespoons butter or olive oil
Salt and fresh ground pepper

Skin chicken. Place chicken in a shallow oven-proof dish. Sprinkle with tarragon vinegar and tarragon leaves. Dot with butter or sprinkle with olive oil. Season to taste. Cover with foil and bake 20 minutes at 350°. Remove foil and bake another 15-20 minutes. Serves 4.

Variations: Substitute 2 Tablespoons chopped fresh basil (1 Tablespoon dried) or 1 Tablespoon fresh thyme (1½ teaspoons dried) for the tarragon.

Chicken Kiev

A very simple dish that can serve as sophisticated fare for a dinner party. Make-up a few hours ahead and place in refrigerator. Pop into the oven when your guests arrive and dinner will cook while you visit.

4 chicken breast halves, skinned and boned
2/3 cup melted butter or margarine
Mix:
1 Tablespoon fresh finely chopped basil (2 t. dried)
2 teaspoons fresh finely chopped oregano (1 t. dried)
1 cup fine dry bread crumbs
2 cloves garlic minced
2 Tablespoons grated parmesan cheese
½ teaspoon salt

Rinse boned and skinned chicken breasts and pat dry. Dip chicken in melted butter. Roll chicken in the bread crumb mix. Roll breasts from the long narrow end and place seam side down in a shallow baking dish.
Mix:
Leftover melted butter
¼ cup dry white wine
½ cup chopped green onions

Pour over chicken. Cover dish and bake at 350° for 30 minutes. Remove cover. Sprinkle with ¼ cup fresh chopped parsley. Continue to bake another 15 minutes until done. Serves 4. Serve with wild rice or fresh garlic pasta.

Chicken Breasts with Brie and Fines Herbes

6 chicken breast halves, skinned and boned
Freshly ground pepper
2 Tablespoons chopped green onions with 2-3" of tops
2 Tablespoons fines herbes (1 Tablespoon dried)
1 clove finely minced garlic
2 Tablespoons butter or margarine, softened
4 ounces of brie cheese, rind removed
2 Tablespoons mayonnaise
½ teaspoon Dijon style mustard
¼ cup white wine

Place chicken breast pieces between 2 pieces of waxed paper. Flatten slightly with flat side of meat hammer. Sprinkle with ground pepper. Mix onions, fines herbes and garlic with softened butter. Spread butter mix on one side of flattened chicken breasts. Cut brie into 2" chunks, soften 10-15 seconds in microwave. Spread brie on chicken breasts. Roll breast pieces from short end and lay seam-side down in shallow baking dish. Spread tops with a mixture of mayonnaise and Dijon mustard. Add wine, cover and bake 350° for 25 minutes. Remove foil and bake another 15 minutes or until done.

Crisp Oven-Fried Chicken

This recipe goes way back to the 70's when my children were very small and wanted fried chicken. I disliked frying anything because of the mess. This substitute was one of their favorites.

1 (3 pound) frying chicken
½ cup unsalted butter or margarine
½ teaspoon onion salt
½ teaspoon Lawry's salt
1 teaspoon dried thyme
1 teaspoon dried marjoram
2-3 cups of crushed potato chips

Rinse chicken and pat dry. Cut into serving-size pieces. Melt butter. Add onion salt, Lawry's salt, thyme and marjoram. Mix well. Dip chicken pieces into butter mixture. Roll in crushed potato chips. Place on a lightly greased cookie sheet. Bake in preheated 375° oven for 45 minutes or until golden brown and cooked through.

Oregano Sour Cream Baked Chicken
This dish can be served hot with a simple pasta,
or cold in a chicken salad.

4 chicken breasts halves
½ cup grated Parmesan or Romano cheese
½ cup mayonnaise
½ cup low-fat homemade sour cream*
2 teaspoons fresh, chopped oregano (1 teaspoon dried)
2 small cloves garlic, finely minced

Mix cheese, mayonnaise, sour cream, oregano and garlic.
Rinse and pat dry chicken breasts. Place breasts in a
baking pan. Pour cheese mixture evenly over chicken.
Bake in preheated 350° for 45 minutes until cooked
through.

*Homemade Low-Fat Sour Cream:

1 pound carton of low-fat, small curd cottage cheese
2 Tablespoons of fresh lemon juice.

Place cottage cheese and lemon juice in blender or food
processor and process until it has the consistency of
commercially prepared sour cream.

Scallops in Asiago Cream

1 pound sea scallops
10-15 new small carrots 3-4" long
5 green onions with 3" of tops, cut into ½" slices
2 Tablespoons olive oil
½ cup half-and-half
2 Tablespoons fresh lemon juice
1 cup fresh spinach cut in strips
1 Tablespoon coarsely chopped basil leaves
½ pound fusilli pasta (spiral shape to hold sauce)
3 Tablespoons asiago cheese (can substitute Romano
   or Parmesan)

Cook carrots in lightly salted water until crisp tender.
Cook fusilli while preparing the following: Sauté scallops
and green onion in olive oil over medium heat. (Scallops
will be more tender if cooked at a medium temperature
just until done.) Remove scallops to a warm bowl. Add
the half and half and cook until reduced slightly. Add
lemon juice, spinach and basil to pan. Cook quickly until
spinach is wilted. Add cooked carrots and scallops. Stir
in cooked pasta and cheese. Serves 4.

Broiled Scallops with Greens

This dish provides a nice contrast for the scallops. It is quick, easy and beautiful for a dinner party.

1½ pounds of scallops
Rinse scallops and place in a 9" x 13" non-aluminum, shallow baking dish.

Marinade:
¼ cup tamari sauce
¼ cup sake
½ cup chopped green onion
½ teaspoon fresh grated ginger

Combine and pour over scallops. Marinate in the refrigerator for 1 hour. Preheat broiler (425°) for 10 minutes. (I use convection broil in rack position #3 at 400°. Broil scallops in the marinade for 6-8 minutes (4-7 in convection). Do not overcook.

Greens:
2 Tablespoons toasted sesame oil
1 Tablespoon butter
2-3 cloves minced garlic
6-8 ounces fresh spinach
6 ounces fresh mustard greens

Remove stems from greens and tear into large bite-size pieces. Heat sesame oil and butter in a large skillet over high heat. Cook garlic for 30 seconds, stirring constantly. Add spinach and greens, stir. Cover and cook for about 2 minutes until wilted. To serve, place scallops and greens over rice. Serves 4.

Steamed Salmon

A simple method for fish preparation – and , oh, so tasty!

4 salmon steaks or filet pieces (6 oz each)
1 cup chicken broth
½ cup dry white wine
Zest from ½ lemon
1 Tablespoon lemon juice
½ carrot thinly sliced
1 stalk celery, finely chopped
2 Tablespoons chopped green onion
1 Tablespoon chopped chives
2 Tablespoons chopped fresh parsley
1 (3") sprig of tarragon
Salt and fresh ground pepper

Season salmon lightly with salt and pepper. Wrap each piece of salmon in parchment paper. Set aside. Combine remaining ingredients in bottom of steamer. Bring to a boil, insert steamer tray with fish pieces. Cover , reduce heat to medium high and steam for 12-15 minutes depending upon thickness of fish pieces. Strain sauce and serve with fish.

Salmon Soufflé for Two

This is so easy. I can't believe I spent so many years being intimidated by soufflés. Give it a try.

2 Tablespoons unsalted butter
1 Tablespoon grated Romano or Parmesan cheese
1 Tablespoon finely chopped green onion
2 Tablespoons flour
½ cup milk
1 teaspoon dijon-style mustard
2 teaspoons lemon juice
2 egg yolks, lightly beaten
¼ cup grated Monterey Jack or Gruyère cheese
1 cup cooked, flaked salmon (I buy one 8 ounce
    frozen salmon steak)
½ teaspoon salt
2 teaspoons chopped parsley
2 teaspoons chopped dill weed
4 large egg whites
½ teaspoon cream of tartar

Place cookie sheet on oven rack in lower third of oven. Preheat oven to 400° (375° for convection oven). Butter a 1 quart soufflé dish with ½ Tablespoon butter. Sprinkle with grated Romano cheese. Place in refrigerator to chill.

Sauté green onions in the remaining butter. Add flour and cook for 2-3 minutes. Heat milk and gradually whisk into flour. Bring to a simmer, whisk in mustard and lemon juice. Cook for 3 minutes. Whisk ¼ cup of the hot mixture into the egg yolks. Add egg mixture to the remaining white sauce in pan. Bring to simmer for 1 minute. Remove from heat and add all remaining ingredients except egg whites and cream of tartar.

While salmon mixture cools, whip egg whites until frothy. Add cream of tartar and gradually increase whipping speed to medium high until *soft peaks* form. Do not over beat egg whites – soft peaks allow the soufflé to rise perfectly. Fold about a ½ cup of the whites into the salmon mixture. Fold in the rest of the whites and place mixture into soufflé dish. To create the crown effect on your soufflé, run a butter knife up and down 1" deep and 1" from the edge of the dish just before placing in the oven. Place soufflé on preheated cookie sheet. If using regular oven, reduce heat to 375°. Bake until golden brown, 30 to 35 minutes. The top should still wiggle a bit when disturbed. Serve immediately. Recipe can be doubled successfully.

HERBAL JELLIES AND DESSERTS

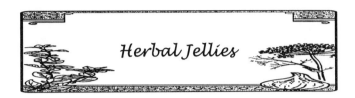

Herbal Jellies

Lavender Jelly

3 cups boiling distilled water (a good
   white wine can be substituted
   for the water)
1 cup fresh lavender tips
4 ½ cups sugar
¼ cup cider vinegar
1 (3 ounce) envelope liquid pectin
6-8 fresh lavender sprigs.

Place lavender tips in stainless steel or ceramic container.
Pour boiling water over and steep for ½ hour. Strain
liquid and measure 2 cups of the lavender "tea" into a
large pan. Add sugar and vinegar. Mix well and bring to
a full rolling boil, stirring constantly. Add pectin and
return to a boil that cannot be stirred down. Boil 1
minute, stirring constantly. Remove from heat and add a
couple drops of blue food color if you wish. Skim foam.
Place an herb sprig in the bottom of sterilized jars. Pour
hot jelly into jars and cover with sterilized lids. Tighten
caps. Place in hat water bath for 10 minutes. (**Rose
Geranium jelly** can be made by substituting 30 rose-
scented geranium leaves for the lavender tips. Or, for
Tarragon jelly, substitute 1 cup of rough-chopped
tarragon leaves.)

Rosemary Garlic Jelly

This jelly is wonderful served with meats

3 cups boiling distilled water (a good red
    wine can be substituted for the water)
1 cup fresh rosemary leaves
4 ½ cups sugar
¼ cup cider vinegar
1 Tablespoon finely minced garlic
1 (3 ounce) envelope liquid pectin
6-8 fresh rosemary sprigs

Place rosemary leaves in stainless steel or ceramic
container. Pour boiling water over and steep for ½ hour.
Strain liquid and measure 2 cups of the rosemary "tea"
into a large pan. Add sugar, vinegar and garlic. Mix well
and bring to a full rolling boil, stirring constantly. Add
pectin and return to a boil that cannot be stirred down.
Boil 1 minute, stirring constantly. Remove from heat.
Skim foam. Place an herb sprig in the bottom of sterilized
jars. Pour hot jelly into jars and cover with sterilized lids.
Tighten caps. Place in hat water bath for 10 minutes.

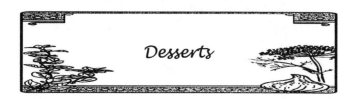

Desserts

Herb Jelly Thumb-Print Cookies

½ cup butter
¼ cup oil
1 ½ cups powdered sugar
¼ teaspoon salt
1 egg
1 teaspoon vanilla
2 cups flour
1 teaspoon baking soda
1 teaspoon cream of tartar
2 Tablespoons fresh or dried lavender flowers
Lavender jelly

Beat together until well blended, butter, oil, powdered
sugar, salt, egg and vanilla. Sift dry ingredients into
butter mixture and mix well. Stir in lavender. Chill
mixture. Preheat oven to 350°. Shape into 1" balls. Bake
2" apart on ungreased cookie sheets. Remove from oven.
Place ½ teaspoon herb jelly in center of cookies.

Minty Chocolate Cookies
A taste sensation!

2 (1 ounce) squares of
   unsweetened baker's chocolate
1 cup unsalted butter
1 cup sugar (can use ½ cup
   brown sugar and ½ cup white)
2 egg yolks
½ teaspoon salt
2 - 2½ cups flour
1 teaspoon vanilla
½ cup finely chopped, toasted pecans
½ cup mint jelly with mint leaves

Melt the chocolate and set aside to cool slightly. Cream
the butter and sugar until light. Beat in the eggs. Mix
the salt with 2 cups of the flour. Add to the creamed
butter mixture and mix well. Add vanilla, pecans and
melted chocolate. Mix well. Add enough additional flour
to make the dough firm. Refrigerate the dough for 1 hour.
Preheat oven to 325°. Break off pieces of dough to make
1" balls. Roll into ball and place on lightly greased cookie
sheets 2" apart. Make a small indentation with your
finger or a small dowel – don't use your thumb, it's too
big. Bake 8 to 10 minutes. Remove from pan and allow to
cool for 5 minutes. Using a small spoon or measuring
spoon, place approximately ¼ teaspoon jelly in the
indentations of each cookie. Sprinkle with cocoa or
powdered sugar.

Lemon Balm Bread

¾ cup milk
2 Tablespoons fresh lemon balm leaves finely chopped
2 Tablespoons fresh lemon thyme leaves finely chopped
1/3 cup softened butter
1 cup sugar
2 eggs
1 ½ Tablespoons finely grated
   and chopped lemon zest
2 cups flour
1 ½ teaspoons baking powder
¼ teaspoon salt

Line a 9x5x3 inch pan with lightly buttered parchment
paper. Preheat oven to 325°. Heat milk with the chopped
herbs and steep until cool. Cream the butter and sugar
until light and fluffy. Add eggs one at a time, beating
well. Add the lemon zest. Sift remaining dry ingredients
into the batter alternately with the herb and milk
mixture, just until blended. Pour batter into prepared
pan and bake for 45-50 minutes. While bread is still
warm, glaze with 1 cup powdered sugar and juice of one
lemon.

A Cooking Heritage

My grandmother was born in Budapest and raised along the banks of the Danube, a stone's throw from the pastries of Vienna. At the age of 15, my grandmother and her mother departed Budapest to meet my great-grandfather in the United States. The trip to America and processing through Ellis Island were emotional and grueling for my rather shy, soft-spoken grandmother. While she brought only meager possessions, she carried a precious legacy, the cuisine of the Danube; a heady commingling  of the Austrian and Hungarian culinary skills that she was to share with her five daughters and their daughters.

A visit to Grandma's included a great serving of stuffed green peppers or goulash with huge chunks of beef laced with paprika, followed by a poppyseed kolachi served with a glass of milk. The lightly sweetened, ground poppy seed mixture was daubed onto a small square of delicate yeast dough, rolled into the shape of a crescent and baked until golden. She used a sinful amount of butter and eggs in the dough.

Those foods are my heritage. The stuffed peppers on the back of the range meant more than mere sustenance. They represented the hospitality that my grandmother extended to all who passed through her kitchen door. It was her simple way of saying, "Welcome. Sit down. Tell me about your world. *I love you.*" Food opened the heart's door to conversation and intimacy.

When our family comes together for Christmas, my two
sisters and I bring our individual interpretations of
Grandma's recipe. We share coffee, sample each other's
kolachi, open our hearts and understand that we are
family.

Poppyseed Kolachi

1 package dry yeast
8 cups flour
1 teaspoon salt
1 cup butter plus ¼ cup
   vegetable shortening
½ cup sugar
2 whole eggs
6 egg yolks
2½ cup milk, divided
1 teaspoon vanilla

Allow yeast to dissolve in ½ cup warm milk and ¼
teaspoon sugar for 10 minutes. Sift flour after measuring.
Make cups level. Add salt to sifting. Cream butter, add
sugar and beat until fluffy. Beat in eggs 2 or 3 at a time.
Beat thoroughly. Add raised yeast and mix. Add flour
alternately with the remaining milk and vanilla. If this is
mixed well in a large basin by hand, no kneading is
necessary. Dough will be very soft. Let rise about 2
hours in warm place. Take out a portion of dough and
work with flour until it can be rolled. Roll out to 1/8"
thickness and cut into 4" squares. Stretch slightly to
make diamond shape, place approximately 1 teaspoon of
one of the following fillings in upper corner of dough. Roll
up as for crescent rolls. Seal edges. Let rise for 15
minutes. Bake at 400° for 15 to 20 minutes. Makes

approximately 4 dozen rolls. Rolls freeze well. Thaw and warm in microwave.

Kolachi Fillings
Canned "Solo" or "Bohemian Kitchen" fillings may be purchased and used directly from the can (prune, poppy, date, etc.). I prefer the following additions to the canned product.

Poppy Seed Filling

1 can poppy filling
1 tablespoon butter
¼ cup sugar
¼ cup water

Mix all ingredients, simmer on low heat for 15 minutes; cool. Add 1 teaspoon vanilla. Fill rolls with approximately 1 full teaspoon.

Nut Filling
2 tablespoons butter
1 cup brown sugar
2 tablespoons cornstarch
½ teaspoon cinnamon
¼ teaspoon salt
2 cups finely-chopped walnuts
1 teaspoon vanilla

Cut butter into sugar, cornstarch, cinnamon and salt. Mix in nuts and vanilla. Fill rolls with approximately 1 full teaspoon of filling.

Rose Geranium Angel Food Cake

Angel cake is an excellent showcase for your lovely rose-scented geranium leaves – with the added bonus of being fat-free and fairly low in calories

1 cup sifted cake flour
1½ cups sifted granulated sugar
13 large egg whites
1 teaspoon cream of tartar
½ teaspoon salt
2 Tablespoons rose flower water
   (available at specialty food shops)
½ teaspoon pure vanilla (clear as
   opposed to dark if available)

Heat oven to 325°. Combine flour with half of sugar. Mix flour and sugar very well with a whisk. Beat egg whites on low speed until frothy. Add cream of tartar and salt. Beat at medium speed until soft billowy mounds form. With mixer running on medium speed, add the sugar, one tablespoon at a time until sugar is incorporated and whites form *soft* peaks. Do not overbeat whites. You do not want them to look dry. They should look shiny and move slightly when the mixing bowl is tipped. Stir in the rose flower water and vanilla. Remove bowl from mixer stand. Place flour and sugar mixture in sifter and gently sift ¼ of the mixture over the egg whites. Using a large spatula or your hand, gently fold the flour into the egg whites making certain that you get to the bottom of the bowl. Continue adding flour in ¼'s until all flour is incorporated. Spoon the batter into a clean, ungreased tube pan with a removable bottom. If your pan does not have a removable bottom, line the bottom with parchment paper. Smooth the top of the batter and rap the pan on a

112

hard surface to release large air pockets. Bake in the lower third of the oven for approximately 1 hour or until the top is golden and springs back slightly from the touch. If your pan has feet, invert it onto the counter and leave until cool. If not, invert over the neck of a heavy bottle. When cool, loosen the cake from the pan and place on serving plate.

Glaze:
½ to 1 cup of rose-scented geranium jelly
1 teaspoon lemon juice
1/8 teaspoon grenadine syrup

Warm the jelly slightly to liquefy it. Add lemon juice and grenadine syrup (for color) and mix well. Drizzle jelly over the cake. Garnish with raspberries and rose geranium leaves that have been "painted" with lightly beaten egg whites and dipped in fine sugar.

Rose Geranium Chiffon Cake

This is the "flip-side" of the angel food cake. Lots more calories, but unbelievably delicious!

1½ cup sugar
1 1/3 cup cake flour
2 teaspoons baking powder
½ teaspoon salt
7 eggs, 2 whole and 5 separated
¾ cup water
½ cup oil
½ Tablespoon vanilla
1 Tablespoon rose flower water
½ teaspoon cream of tartar

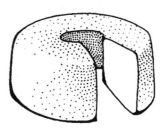

Preheat oven to 325° and move rack to lower 1/3 of oven. Measure sugar, flour baking powder and salt into large mixing bowl and whisk to mix and fluff. Add two eggs, 5 egg yolks, water, oil, vanilla and rose flower water. Beat egg whites on medium speed until foamy . Add cream of tartar and beat on medium-high until whites are very stiff. Fold whites into flour mixture until well blended. Pour into 9" ungreased tube pan. Bake for 50-60 minutes or until tester comes out clean and cake springs back slightly to the touch. Remove pan from oven, invert on counter until cool. Glaze the same as Rose-Geranium Angel Food Cake.

PET
PANTRY

Dog Biscuits

Angus Biscuits

These biscuits are an all out favorite of our Chocolate Labrador Retriever, Angus. He is not very particular about his food however, so don't use him as a gauge.

½ pound of beef liver, chopped fine and cooked
4 large carrots, chopped and cooked with the liver
4 cloves fresh garlic pressed and cooked with
   the carrot and liver
1 Tablespoon dry yeast
½ cup warm water
1 teaspoon honey
3 cups flour
2 cups whole wheat flour
2 cups stone ground cornmeal
1½ cups rolled oats
1 cup powdered milk
½ cup wheat germ
½ cup brewer's yeast
2 teaspoons salt
4 eggs beaten

Preheat oven to 300°. Place liver, carrots, garlic and cooking water in food processor and process until smooth. Dissolve the yeast in the warm water and honey. Blend all dry ingredients together in a large bowl. Stir the liver mixture, yeast and eggs together and add to the dry ingredients. Mix well, adding enough additional liquid to

116

make a firm dough. Knead for four minutes. Allow dough to rest. Divide dough into four pieces. Roll out to 3/8" thickness, cut shapes with cookie cutter or cut into squares. Place on lightly greased cookie sheets and pierce each biscuit a few times with fork tines. Biscuits can be brushed with broth or egg before baking. Put as many cookie sheets in oven as will fit. Remaining biscuits can be refrigerated or frozen until baked. Bake for 1 hour. Turn off the oven and leave biscuits in the oven for several hours until crispy dry. *This makes a large batch. I usually make them in the morning so that I can bake a second batch in the evening to leave in the oven overnight.*

Allergy-Free Dog Biscuits

This recipe has been adapted by my friend Kathy Johnson to make it acceptable for dogs that may have allergies. Those changes have been noted by an OR in the text. Most flours can be found at natural food stores.

2 cups flour
   OR

½ cup rice flour	½ cup potato flour
½ cup oat flour	½ cup graham flour

1 cup cornmeal
2/3 cup brewer's yeast
2 teaspoons garlic powder
   OR: 3-4 fresh garlic cloves, pressed
½ teaspoon salt (optional)
2 egg yolks
   OR: egg substitute
2 Tablespoons olive oil
3 chicken or beef bouillon cubes
   dissolved in 1½ cups water
One jar of junior baby food meat meals (optional).

Mix all ingredients well. Roll out half of dough to 3/8"
thickness. Cut shapes with cookie cutter or cut into
squares. Repeat with other half of dough. Pierce each
biscuit with baking fork. Brush biscuits with a little
broth if desired. Bake at 375° for 30 minutes. Turn off
oven and leave biscuits in oven until cool.

Aïoli, 39
Appetizers, 33
   Herbal Cheesecake, 33
   Herbed Cheeses in Seasoned Oil, 35
   Marinated Feta Cheese, 34
   Seasoned French Bread, 36
Balsamic Vinaigrette, 49
Basil Cheese Spread, 42
Basil Pesto Bread, 66
Basil Zucchini, 55
Beef Stew, 89
Beverages, 27
   Bishop Saint Nicholas Punch, 32
   Easy May Wine, 30
   Herb Syrups, 31
   herbal tea, 28
   May Wine, 30
   Melissa Root Tea, 29
Bishop Saint Nicholas Punch, 32
Bouquet Garni, 23
Boursin, Mocq, 42
Bowtie Pasta with Fresh Salmon, 74
Breads, 64
   Basil Pesto Bread Variation, 66
   Corn Muffins, Hot-Dilled, 69
   Flowerpot Herbed Bread, 67
   Focaccia, 68
   Herb Waffles, 70
   Herbes de Provence Sourdough Bread, 64
   Savory Herb Bread, 65
Broiled Scallops with Greens, 99
Butter Italia, 38
Butter of Provence, 39
Cakes
   Rose Geranium Angel Food, 112
   Rose Geranium Chiffon, 114
Carrots, Minted Baby, 59
Cheese and Garlic Pasta, 73
Chicken Breasts with Brie and Fines Herbes, 95
Chicken Kiev, 94
Chicken Salad, Mediterranean, 47
Chicken Wing Soup, 76
Chive Butter, 37

Chive Flower Cheese Spread, 41
Chive Sauce, 50
Citrus Salad Dressing, 49
Classic Herbes de Provençe, 22
clostridium botulinum, 19
Corn Muffins, Hot-Dilled, 69
Cream of Brie and Leek Soup, 79
Cream Puff, Savory, 81
Crisp Oven-Fried Chicken, 96
Cucumber Sandwiches, 43
Curry Dip, 41
Dog Biscuits
   Allergy-Free, 117
   Angus Biscuits, 116
Easy May Wine, 30
Fines Herbes, 22
Flowerpot Herbed Bread, 67
Focaccia, 68
French Tarragon Butter, 38
Fresh Herbs and Pasta, 73
Fresh Marinated Vegetables, 53
Fresh Mozzarella Pizza, 82
Fresh Tomato Pasta, 58
Garlic, Roasted, 60
Golden Baked Tomatoes and Zucchini, 55
Grilled Marinated Vegetables, 52
Harvesting and Preserving Herbs, 14
   Convection Oven Drying, 15
   Drying, 14
   Freezing, 16
   Microwave Drying, 14
Herb Butters
   Butter Italia, 38
   Chive, 37
   French Tarragon, 38
Herb Butters and Spreads, 37
   Aïoli, 39
   Basil Cheese Spread, 42
   Boursin, Mocq, 42
   Butter of Provence, 39
   Chive Flower Cheese Spread, 41
   Herbed Mustard, 40
   Liver Pate, 43
   Provencal Cheese Spread, 40

Herb Jelly Thumb Print Cookies, 106
Herb Syrups, 31
Herb Vinaigrette, 46
Herb Waffles, 70
Herbal Cheesecake, 33
Herbal Infused Oils, 19
herbal tea, 28
Herbed Cheeses in Seasoned Oil, 35
Herbed Mustard, 40
Herbed Pork Roast, 91
Herbed Vinegars, 17
Herbes de Provence Sourdough Bread, 64
Herbes de Provençe, 23, 34
    My Favorite, 23
Holiday Roast Beef, 88
Jellies, 104
    Lavender Jelly, 104
    Rose Geranium Jelly, 104
    Rosemary Garlic Jelly, 105
    Tarragon, 104
Kale with Marjoram, 56
Kolachi, 110
Kolachi Fillings, 111
Lavender Jelly, 104
Lemon Balm Bread, 108
Liver Pâté, 43
Marinated Feta Cheese Appetizer, 34
May Wine, 30
Meat, 88
    Beef
        Holiday Roast Beef, 88
        Meat Loaf, 90
        Stew, 89
    Lamb
        Rosemary Roasted Lamb, 92
    Pork
        Herbed Pork Roast, 91
Meat Loaf, 90
Melissa Root Tea, 29
Minted Baby Carrots, 59
Minty Chocolate Cookies, 107
Omelette Casserole, 86

Oregano Pesto, 26
Oregano Sour Cream Baked Chicken, 97
Oregon State University
    herbal infused oils, 19
Pasta Dough Basic, 71
Pastas, 71
    Basic Pasta Dough, 71
    Bowtie Pasta with Fresh Salmon, 74
    Cheese and Garlic Pasta, 73
    Fresh Herbs and Pasta, 73
Peppers, Roasted, 61
Pesto, 25
    Basil, 25
    Mint, 26
    Oregano Pesto, 26
Pizza, 82
Poppyseed Kolachi, 110
Pork Medallion Sage Sauce, 50
Poultry
    Chicken Breasts with Brie and Fines Herbes, 95
    Chicken Kiev, 94
    Crisp Oven-Fried Chicken, 96
    Oregano Sour Cream Baked Chicken, 97
    Tarragon Chicken Bake, 93
Provençal Cheese Spread, 40
Quiche Lorraine, 84
Raspberry Vinegar Salad Dressing, 48
Roasted Garlic, 60
Roasted Garlic Salad Dressing, 48
Rose Geranium Angel Food Cake, 112
Rose Geranium Chiffon Cake, 114
Rose Geranium Jelly, 104
Rosemary Garlic Jelly, 105
Rosemary Roasted Lamb, 92
Rosemary Spinach Bake, 54
Salad Herb Blend, 24
Salad of Herbs, 46
Salads, Dressings and Sauces, 45
    A Salad of Herbs, 46
    Balsamic Vinaigrette, 49
    Chicken Salad, Mediterranean, 47
    Chive Sauce, 50

Citrus Salad Dressing, 49
Herb Vinaigrette, 46
Pork Medallion Sage Sauce, 50
Raspberry Vinegar Salad Dressing, 48
Roasted Garlic Salad Dressing, 48
Tomato and Basil Salad, 47
Salmon Soufflé for Two, 101
Santa Fe Cheese Soup, 77
Savory Herb Bread, 65
Savory Pâte à Choux, 81
Scallops in Asiago Cream, 98
Seafood
Bowtie Pasta with Fresh Salmon, 74
Broiled Scallops with Greens, 99
Salmon Soufflé for Two, 101
Scallops in Asiago Cream, 98
Steamed Salmon, 100
Seasoned French Bread, 36
Shrimp Dip, 44
Soups, 76
Chicken Wing Soup, 76
Cream of Brie and Leek Soup, 79
Santa Fe Cheese Soup, 77

Tomato, Chilled, 80
Spaghetti, Polish, 83
Steamed Salmon, 100
Stocking Your Spice Cabinet, 21
Basil Pesto, 25
Bouquet Garni, 23
Classic Herbes de Provence, 22
Fines Herbes, 22
Mint Pesto, 26
Oregano Pesto, 26
Salad Herb Blend, 24
Stuffed Onions, 57
Swiss Chard, 59
Tarragon Chicken Bake, 93
Tarragon Jelly, 104
Tomato and Basil Salad, 47
Tomato Sauce, Roasted Garlic and Peppers, 62
Tomato Soup, Chilled, 80
Tomato Zucchini Sauté, 56
Vegetables, 51
Welsh Rarebit, 87

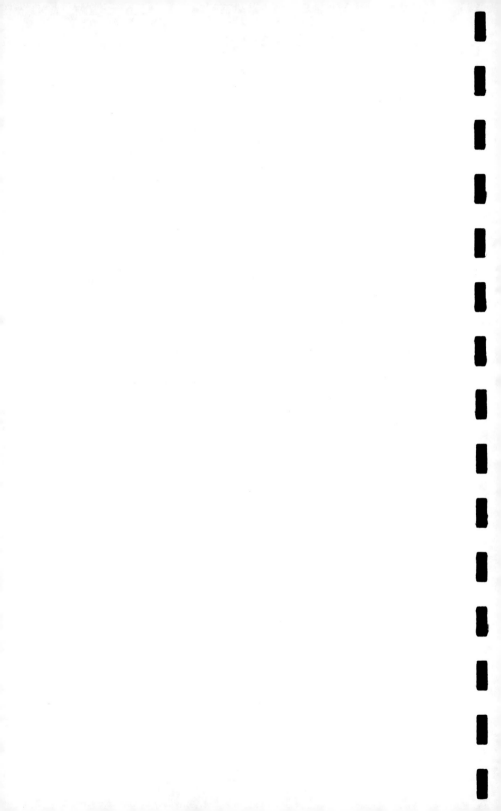

Need a Gift?

for

• Shower • Birthday • Mother's Day •
• Anniversary • Christmas•

Turn Page For Order Form
(Order Now While Supply Lasts!)

To Order Copies

Please send me _____ copies
at $9.95 each. (Make checks payable
to **QUIXOTE PRESS**.)

Name _____

Street _____

City _____ State _____ Zip _____

Send Orders To:

Quixote Press
3544 Blakeslee St.
Wever, IA 52658

- -

To Order Copies

Please send me _____ copies
at $9.95 each. (Make checks payable
to **QUIXOTE PRESS**.)

Name _____

Street _____

City _____ State _____ Zip _____

Send Orders To:

Quixote Press
3544 Blakeslee St.
Wever, IA 52658

Since you have enjoyed this book, perhaps you would be interested in some of these others from QUIXOTE PRESS.

ARKANSAS BOOKS

HOW TO TALK ARKANSAS
    by Bruce Carlson .... paperback $7.95
ARKANSAS' ROADKILL COOKBOOK
    by Bruce Carlson .... paperback $7.95
REVENGE OF ROADKILL
    by Bruce Carlson .... paperback $7.95
GHOSTS OF THE OZARKS
    by Bruce Carlson .... paperback $9.95
THE BEST OF THE MISSISSIPPI RIVER GHOST STORIES
    by Bruce Carlson .... paperback $9.95
LET'S US GO DOWN TO THE RIVER 'N . . .
    by various authors .... paperback $9.95
ARKANSAS' VANISHING OUTHOUSE
    by Bruce Carlson .... paperback $9.95
TALL TALES OF THE MISSISSIPPI RIVER
    by Dan Titus .... paperback $9.95
LOST & BURIED TREASURE OF THE MISSISSIPPI RIVER
    by Netha Bell & Gary Scholl .... paperback $9.95
TALES OF HACKETT'S CREEK
    by Dan Titus .... paperback $9.95
THE LI'L RED BOOK OF FISHIN' TIPS
    by Tom Whitecloud .... paperback $7.95
101 WAYS TO USE A DEAD RIVER FLY
    by Bruce Carlson .... paperback $7.95
VACANT LOT, SCHOOL YARD & BACK ALLEY GAMES
    by various authors .... paperback $9.95
HOW TO TALK MIDWESTERN
    by Robert Thomas .... paperback $7.95
ARKANSAS COOKIN'
    by Bruce Carlson .... (3x5) paperback $5.95
ANIMAL PESTS & HOW TO GET THE UPPER HAND ON 'EM
    by S. Meyer .... paperback $9.95
THE ~~ROAD~~ AIRPLANE KILL COOKBOOK
    by Bruce Carlson .... paperback $7.95
OUT BEHIND THE BARN
    by Bruce Carlson .... paperback $9.95
TRAINS WEST
    by Carole Johnston .... paperback $9.95
KID MONEY (how little bitty kids can earn money)
    by Bev Faaborg .... paperback $5.95

DAKOTA BOOKS

THE LI'L RED BOOK OF FISHIN' TIPS
    by Tom Whitecloud .... paperback $7.95
Some Pretty Tame, but Kinda Funny Stories About Early
DAKOTA LADIES-OF-THE-EVENING
    by Bruce Carlson .... paperback $9.95

SOUTH DAKOTA ROADKILL COOKBOOK
by Bruce Carlson .... paperback $7.95
REVENGE OF ROADKILL
by Bruce Carlson .... paperback $7.95
101 WAYS TO USE A DEAD RIVER FLY
by Bruce Carlson .... paperback $7.95
LET'S US GO DOWN TO THE RIVER 'N . . .
by various authors .... paperback $9.95
LOST & BURIED TREASURE OF THE MISSOURI RIVER
by Netha Bell .... paperback $9.95
MAKIN' DO IN SOUTH DAKOTA
by various authors .... paperback $9.95
THE DAKOTAS' VANISHING OUTHOUSE
by Bruce Carlson .... paperback $9.95
VACANT LOT, SCHOOL YARD & BACK ALLEY GAMES
by various authors .... paperback $9.95
HOW TO TALK MIDWESTERN
by Robert Thomas .... paperback $7.95
DAKOTA COOKIN'
by Bruce Carlson .... (3x5) paperback $5.95
ANIMAL PESTS & HOW TO GET THE UPPER HAND ON 'EM
by S. Meyer .... paperback $9.95
THE ROAD AIRPLANE KILL COOKBOOK
by Bruce Carlson .... paperback $7.95
OUT BEHIND THE BARN
by Bruce Carlson .... paperback $9.95
TRAINS WEST
by Carole Johnston .... paperback $9.95
KID MONEY (how little bitty kids can earn money)
by Bev Faaborg .... paperback $5.95

ILLINOIS BOOKS

ILLINOIS COOKIN'
by Bruce Carlson .... (3x5) paperback $5.95
THE VANISHING OUTHOUSE OF ILLINOIS
by Bruce Carlson .... paperback $9.95
A FIELD GUIDE TO ILLINOIS' CRITTERS
by Bruce Carlson .... paperback $7.95
Some Pretty Tame, but Kinda Funny Stories About Early
ILLINOIS LADIES-OF-THE-EVENING
by Bruce Carlson .... paperback $9.95
ILLINOIS' ROADKILL COOKBOOK
by Bruce Carlson .... paperback $7.95
101 WAYS TO USE A DEAD RIVER FLY
by Bruce Carlson .... paperback $7.95
TALL TALES OF THE MISSISSIPPI RIVER
by Dan Titus .... paperback $9.95
TALES OF HACKETT'S CREEK
by Dan Titus .... paperback $9.95
LOST & BURIED TREASURE OF THE MISSISSIPPI RIVER
by Netha Bell & Gary Scholl .... paperback $9.95

STRANGE FOLKS ALONG THE MISSISSIPPI
by Pat Wallace.. paperback $9.95
LET'S US GO DOWN TO THE RIVER 'N . . .
by various authors... paperback $9.95
MISSISSIPPI RIVER PO' FOLK
by Pat Wallace.. paperback $9.95
THE BEST OF THE MISSISSIPPI RIVER GHOST STORIES
by Bruce Carlson... paperback $9.95
THE LI'L RED BOOK OF FISHIN' TIPS
by Tom Whitecloud... paperback $7.95
MAKIN' DO IN ILLINOIS
by various authors... paperback $9.95
MY VERY FIRST
by various authors... paperback $9.95
VACANT LOT, SCHOOL YARD & BACK ALLEY GAMES
by various authors... paperback $9.95
HOW TO TALK MIDWESTERN
by Robert Thomas.. paperback $7.95
ANIMAL PESTS & HOW TO GET THE UPPER HAND ON 'EM
by S. Meyer... paperback $9.95
THE ~~ROAD~~ AIRPLANE KILL COOKBOOK
by Bruce Carlson... paperback $7.95
OUT BEHIND THE BARN
by Bruce Carlson... paperback $9.95
TRAINS WEST
by Carole Johnston... paperback $9.95
KID MONEY (how little bitty kids can earn money)
by Bev Faaborg... paperback $5.95

INDIANA BOOKS

HOW TO TALK INDIANA... paperback $7.95
INDIANA'S ROADKILL COOKBOOK
by Bruce Carlson... paperback $7.95
REVENGE OF ROADKILL
by Bruce Carlson... paperback $7.95
THE LI'L RED BOOK OF FISHIN' TIPS
by Tom Whitecloud... paperback $7.95
GHOSTS OF THE OHIO RIVER (from Cincinnati to Louisville)
by Bruce Carlson... paperback $9.95
LET'S US GO DOWN TO THE RIVER 'N . . .
by various authors... paperback $9.95
101 WAYS TO USE A DEAD RIVER FLY
by Bruce Carlson... paperback $7.95
INDIANA'S VANISHING OUTHOUSE
by Bruce Carlson... paperback $9.95
VACANT LOT, SCHOOL YARD & BACK ALLEY GAMES
by various authors... paperback $9.95
HOW TO TALK MIDWESTERN
by Robert Thomas.. paperback $7.95
INDIANA COOKING
by Bruce Carlson... paperback $5.95

ANIMAL PESTS & HOW TO GET THE UPPER HAND ON 'EM
        by S. Meyer .... paperback $9.95
THE ROAD AIRPLANE KILL COOKBOOK
        by Bruce Carlson .... paperback $7.95
OUT BEHIND THE BARN
        by Bruce Carlson .... paperback $9.95
TRAINS WEST
        by Carole Johnston .... paperback $9.95
KID MONEY (how little bitty kids can earn money)
        by Bev Faaborg .... paperback $5.95

IOWA BOOKS

IOWA COOKIN'
        by Bruce Carlson .... (3x5) paperback $5.95
IOWA'S ROADKILL COOKBOOK
        by Bruce Carlson .... paperback $7.95
REVENGE OF ROADKILL
        by Bruce Carlson .... paperback $7.95
IOWA'S OLD SCHOOLHOUSES
        by Carole Turner Johnston .... paperback $9.95
GHOSTS OF THE AMANA COLONIES
        by Lori Erickson .... paperback $9.95
GHOSTS OF THE IOWA GREAT LAKES
        by Bruce Carlson .... paperback $9.95
THE BEST OF THE MISSISSIPPI RIVER GHOST STORIES
        by Bruce Carlson .... paperback $9.95
GHOSTS OF POLK COUNTY, IOWA
        by Tom Welch .... paperback $9.95
THE LI'L RED BOOK OF FISHIN' TIPS
        by Tom Whitecloud .... paperback $7.95
TALES OF HACKETT'S CREEK
        by Dan Titus .... paperback $9.95
TALL TALES OF THE MISSISSIPPI RIVER
        by Dan Titus .... paperback $9.95
101 WAYS TO USE A DEAD RIVER FLY
        by Bruce Carlson .... paperback $7.95
LET'S US GO DOWN TO THE RIVER 'N . . .
        by various authors .... paperback $9.95
IOWA, THE LAND BETWEEN THE VOWELS
(farm boy stories from the early 1900s)
        by Bruce Carlson .... paperback $9.95
LOST & BURIED TREASURE OF THE MISSISSIPPI RIVER
        by Netha Bell & Gary Scholl .... paperback $9.95
Some Pretty Tame, but Kinda Funny Stories About Early
IOWA LADIES-OF-THE-EVENING
        by Bruce Carlson .... paperback $9.95
IOWA - A JOURNEY IN A PROMISED LAND
        by Kathy Yoder .... paperback $16.95
LOST & BURIED TREASURE OF THE MISSOURI RIVER
        by Netha Bell .... paperback $9.95
FIELD GUIDE TO IOWA'S CRITTERS
        by Bruce Carlson .... paperback $7.95

OLD IOWA HOUSES, YOUNG LOVES
    by Bruce Carlson .... paperback $9.95
SKUNK RIVER ANTHOLOGY
    by Gene Olson .... paperback $9.95
VACANT LOT, SCHOOL YARD & BACK ALLEY GAMES
    by various authors .... paperback $9.95
HOW TO TALK MIDWESTERN
    by Robert Thomas .... paperback $7.95
ANIMAL PESTS & HOW TO GET THE UPPER HAND ON 'EM
    by S. Meyer .... paperback $9.95
THE ROAD AIRPLANE KILL COOKBOOK
    by Bruce Carlson .... paperback $7.95
OUT BEHIND THE BARN
    by Bruce Carlson .... paperback $9.95
TRAINS WEST
    by Carole Johnston .... paperback $9.95
KID MONEY (how little bitty kids can earn money)
    by Bev Faaborg .... paperback $5.95

KANSAS BOOKS

KANSAS COOKING
    by Bruce Carlson .... (3x5) paperback $5.95
STOPOVER IN KANSAS
    by Jon McAlpin .... paperback $9.95
LET'S US GO DOWN TO THE RIVER 'N . . .
    by various authors .... paperback $9.95
LOST & BURIED TREASURE OF THE MISSOURI RIVER
    by Netha Bell .... paperback $9.95
101 WAYS TO USE A DEAD RIVER FLY
    by Bruce Carlson .... paperback $7.95
VACANT LOT, SCHOOL YARD & BACK ALLEY GAMES
    by various authors .... paperback $9.95
HOW TO TALK MIDWESTERN
    by Robert Thomas .... paperback $7.95
ANIMAL PESTS & HOW TO GET THE UPPER HAND ON 'EM
    by S. Meyer .... paperback $9.95
THE ROAD AIRPLANE KILL COOKBOOK
    by Bruce Carlson .... paperback $7.95
OUT BEHIND THE BARN
    by Bruce Carlson .... paperback $9.95
TRAINS WEST
    by Carole Johnston .... paperback $9.95
KID MONEY (how little bitty kids can earn money)
    by Bev Faaborg .... paperback $5.95

KENTUCKY BOOKS

GHOSTS OF THE OHIO RIVER (from Pittsburgh to Cincinnati)
    by Bruce Carlson .... paperback $9.95
GHOSTS OF THE OHIO RIVER (from Cincinnati to Louisville)
    by Bruce Carlson .... paperback $9.95

TALES OF HACKETT'S CREEK
     by Dan Titus .... paperback $9.95
LOST & BURIED TREASURE OF THE MISSISSIPPI RIVER
     by Netha Bell & Gary Scholl .... paperback $9.95
LET'S US GO DOWN TO THE RIVER 'N . . .
     by various authors .... paperback $9.95
UNSOLVED MYSTERIES OF THE MISSISSIPPI
     by Netha Bell .... paperback $9.95
101 WAYS TO USE A DEAD RIVER FLY
     by Bruce Carlson .... paperback $7.95
TALL TALES OF THE MISSISSIPPI RIVER
     by Dan Titus .... paperback $9.95
MY VERY FIRST
     by various authors .... paperback $9.95
VACANT LOT, SCHOOL YARD & BACK ALLEY GAMES
     by various authors .... paperback $9.95
THE LI'L RED BOOK OF FISHIN' TIPS
     by Tom Whitecloud .... paperback $7.95
ANIMAL PESTS & HOW TO GET THE UPPER HAND ON 'EM
     by S. Meyer .... paperback $9.95
THE ROAD AIRPLANE KILL COOKBOOK
     by Bruce Carlson .... paperback $7.95
OUT BEHIND THE BARN
     by Bruce Carlson .... paperback $9.95
TRAINS WEST
     by Carole Johnston .... paperback $9.95
KID MONEY (how little bitty kids can earn money)
     by Bev Faaborg .... paperback $5.95

MICHIGAN BOOKS

MICHIGAN COOKIN'
     by Bruce Carlson .... (3x5) paperback $5.95
MICHIGAN'S ROADKILL COOKBOOK
     by Bruce Carlson .... paperback $7.95
MICHIGAN'S VANISHING OUTHOUSE
     by Bruce Carlson .... paperback $9.95
THE LI'L RED BOOK OF FISHIN' TIPS
     by Tom Whitecloud .... paperback $7.95
ANIMAL PESTS & HOW TO GET THE UPPER HAND ON 'EM
     by S. Meyer .... paperback $9.95
THE ROAD AIRPLANE KILL COOKBOOK
     by Bruce Carlson .... paperback $7.95
OUT BEHIND THE BARN
     by Bruce Carlson .... paperback $9.95
TRAINS WEST
     by Carole Johnston .... paperback $9.95
KID MONEY (how little bitty kids can earn money)
     by Bev Faaborg .... paperback $5.95

MINNESOTA BOOKS

MINNESOTA'S ROADKILL COOKBOOK
    by Bruce Carlson .... paperback $7.95
REVENGE OF ROADKILL
    by Bruce Carlson .... paperback $7.95
A FIELD GUIDE TO SMALL MINNESOTA FEMALES
    by Bruce Carlson .... paperback $9.95
THE BEST OF THE MISSISSIPPI RIVER GHOST STORIES
    by Bruce Carlson .... paperback $9.95
LAKES COUNTRY COOKBOOK
    by Bruce Carlson .... paperback $11.95
TALES OF HACKETT'S CREEK
    by Dan Titus .... paperback $9.95
THE LI'L RED BOOK OF FISHIN' TIPS
    by Tom Whitecloud .... paperback $7.95
HOW TO TALK LIKE A MINNESOTA NATIVE .... paperback $7.95
MINNESOTA'S VANISHING OUTHOUSE
    by Bruce Carlson .... paperback $9.95
TALL TALES OF THE MISSISSIPPI RIVER
    by Dan Titus .... paperback $9.95
Some Pretty Tame, but Kinda Funny Stories About Early
MINNESOTA LADIES-OF-THE-EVENING
    by Bruce Carlson .... paperback $9.95
101 WAYS TO USE A DEAD RIVER FLY
    by Bruce Carlson .... paperback $7.95
LOST & BURIED TREASURE OF THE MISSISSIPPI RIVER
    by Netha Bell & Gary Scholl .... paperback $9.95
VACANT LOT, SCHOOL YARD & BACK ALLEY GAMES
    by various authors .... paperback $9.95
HOW TO TALK MIDWESTERN
    by Robert Thomas .... paperback $7.95
MINNESOTA COOKIN'
    by Bruce Carlson .... (3x5) paperback $5.95
ANIMAL PESTS & HOW TO GET THE UPPER HAND ON 'EM
    by S. Meyer .... paperback $9.95
THE ~~ROAD~~ AIRPLANE KILL COOKBOOK
    by Bruce Carlson .... paperback $7.95
OUT BEHIND THE BARN
    by Bruce Carlson .... paperback $9.95
TRAINS WEST
    by Carole Johnston .... paperback $9.95
KID MONEY (how little bitty kids can earn money)
    by Bev Faaborg .... paperback $5.95

MISSOURI BOOKS

MISSOURI COOKIN'
    by Bruce Carlson .... (3x5) paperback $5.95
MISSOURI'S ROADKILL COOKBOOK
    by Bruce Carlson .... paperback $7.95

REVENGE OF ROADKILL
   by Bruce Carlson .... paperback $7.95
LET'S US GO DOWN TO THE RIVER 'N . . .
   by various authors .... paperback $9.95
LAKES COUNTRY COOKBOOK
   by Bruce Carlson .... paperback $11.95
101 WAYS TO USE A DEAD RIVER FLY
   by Bruce Carlson .... paperback $7.95
TALL TALES OF THE MISSISSIPPI RIVER
   by Dan Titus .... paperback $9.95
TALES OF HACKETT'S CREEK
   by Dan Titus .... paperback $9.95
STRANGE FOLKS ALONG THE MISSISSIPPI
   by Pat Wallace .... paperback $9.95
LOST & BURIED TREASURE OF THE MISSOURI RIVER
   by Netha Bell .... paperback $9.95
HOW TO TALK MISSOURIAN
   by Bruce Carlson .... paperback $7.95
VACANT LOT, SCHOOL YARD & BACK ALLEY GAMES
   by various authors .... paperback $9.95
HOW TO TALK MIDWESTERN
   by Robert Thomas .... paperback $7.95
LOST & BURIED TREASURE OF THE MISSISSIPPI RIVER
   by Netha Bell & Gary Scholl .... paperback $9.95
MISSISSIPPI RIVER PO' FOLK
   by Pat Wallace .... paperback $9.95
Some Pretty Tame, but Kinda Funny Stories About Early
MISSOURI LADIES-OF-THE-EVENING
   by Bruce Carlson .... paperback $9.95
THE VANISHING OUTHOUSE OF MISSOURI
   by Bruce Carlson .... paperback $9.95
A FIELD GUIDE TO MISSOURI'S CRITTERS
   by Bruce Carlson .... paperback $7.95
GHOSTS OF THE OZARKS
   by Bruce Carlson .... paperback $9.95
MISSISSIPPI RIVER COOKIN' BOOK
   by Bruce Carlson .... paperback $11.95
MISSOURI'S OLD HOUSES, AND NEW LOVES
   by Bruce Carlson .... paperback $9.95
UNDERGROUND MISSOURI
   by Bruce Carlson .... paperback $9.95
THE LI'L RED BOOK OF FISHIN' TIPS
   by Tom Whitecloud .... paperback $7.95
THE BEST OF THE MISSISSIPPI RIVER GHOST STORIES
   by Bruce Carlson .... paperback $9.95
ANIMAL PESTS & HOW TO GET THE UPPER HAND ON 'EM
   by S. Meyer .... paperback $9.95
THE ROAD AIRPLANE KILL COOKBOOK
   by Bruce Carlson .... paperback $7.95

OUT BEHIND THE BARN
by Bruce Carlson .... paperback $9.95
TRAINS WEST
by Carole Johnston .... paperback $9.95
KID MONEY (how little bitty kids can earn money)
by Bev Faaborg .... paperback $5.95

NEBRASKA BOOKS

LOST & BURIED TREASURE OF THE MISSOURI RIVER
by Netha Bell .... paperback $9.95
101 WAYS TO USE A DEAD RIVER FLY
by Bruce Carlson .... paperback $7.95
LET'S US GO DOWN TO THE RIVER 'N . . .
by various authors .... paperback $9.95
HOW TO TALK MIDWESTERN
by Robert Thomas .... paperback $7.95
VACANT LOT, SCHOOL YARD & BACK ALLEY GAMES
by various authors .... paperback $9.95
THE LI'L RED BOOK OF FISHIN' TIPS
by Tom Whitecloud .... paperback $7.95
ANIMAL PESTS & HOW TO GET THE UPPER HAND ON 'EM
by S. Meyer .... paperback $9.95
THE ROAD AIRPLANE KILL COOKBOOK
by Bruce Carlson .... paperback $7.95
OUT BEHIND THE BARN
by Bruce Carlson .... paperback $9.95
TRAINS WEST
by Carole Johnston .... paperback $9.95
KID MONEY (how little bitty kids can earn money)
by Bev Faaborg .... paperback $5.95

TENNESSEE BOOKS

TALES OF HACKETT'S CREEK
by Dan Titus .... paperback $9.95
TALL TALES OF THE MISSISSIPPI RIVER
by Dan Titus .... paperback $9.95
THE LI'L RED BOOK OF FISHIN' TIPS
by Tom Whitecloud .... paperback $7.95
LOST & BURIED TREASURE OF THE MISSISSIPPI RIVER
by Netha Bell & Gary Scholl .... paperback $9.95
LET'S US GO DOWN TO THE RIVER 'N . . .
by various authors .... paperback $9.95
101 WAYS TO USE A DEAD RIVER FLY
by Bruce Carlson .... paperback $7.95
VACANT LOT, SCHOOL YARD & BACK ALLEY GAMES
by various authors .... paperback $9.95
ANIMAL PESTS & HOW TO GET THE UPPER HAND ON 'EM
by S. Meyer .... paperback $9.95
THE ROAD AIRPLANE KILL COOKBOOK
by Bruce Carlson .... paperback $7.95

OUT BEHIND THE BARN
by Bruce Carlson .... paperback $9.95
TRAINS WEST
by Carole Johnston .... paperback $9.95
KID MONEY (how little bitty kids can earn money)
by Bev Faaborg .... paperback $5.95

WISCONSIN BOOKS

HOW TO TALK WISCONSIN .... paperback $7.95
WISCONSIN COOKIN'
by Bruce Carlson .... (3x5) paperback $5.95
WISCONSIN'S ROADKILL COOKBOOK
by Bruce Carlson .... paperback $7.95
REVENGE OF ROADKILL
by Bruce Carlson .... paperback $7.95
TALL TALES OF THE MISSISSIPPI RIVER
by Dan Titus .... paperback $9.95
THE LI'L RED BOOK OF FISHIN' TIPS
by Tom Whitecloud .... paperback $7.95
LAKES COUNTRY COOKBOOK
by Bruce Carlson .... paperback $11.95
TALES OF HACKETT'S CREEK
by Dan Titus .... paperback $9.95
LET'S US GO DOWN TO THE RIVER 'N . . .
by various authors .... paperback $9.95
101 WAYS TO USE A DEAD RIVER FLY
by Bruce Carlson .... paperback $7.95
UNSOLVED MYSTERIES OF THE MISSISSIPPI
by Netha Bell .... paperback $9.95
LOST & BURIED TREASURE OF THE MISSISSIPPI RIVER
by Netha Bell & Gary Scholl .... paperback $9.95
GHOSTS OF THE MISSISSIPPI RIVER (from Dubuque to Keokuk)
by Bruce Carlson .... paperback $9.95
HOW TO TALK MIDWESTERN
by Robert Thomas .... paperback $7.95
VACANT LOT, SCHOOL YARD & BACK ALLEY GAMES
by various authors .... paperback $9.95
MY VERY FIRST
by various authors .... paperback $9.95
EARLY WISCONSIN HOME REMEDIES
by various authors .... paperback $9.95
THE VANISHING OUTHOUSE OF WISCONSIN
by Bruce Carlson .... paperback $9.95
GHOSTS OF DOOR COUNTY, WISCONSIN
by Geri Rider .... paperback $9.95
Some Pretty Tame, but Kinda Funny Stories About Early
WISCONSIN LADIES-OF-THE-EVENING
by Bruce Carlson .... paperback $9.95
THE BEST OF THE MISSISSIPPI RIVER GHOST STORIES
by Bruce Carlson .... paperback $9.95

ANIMAL PESTS & HOW TO GET THE UPPER HAND ON 'EM
by S. Meyer .... paperback $9.95
THE ROAD AIRPLANE KILL COOKBOOK
by Bruce Carlson .... paperback $7.95
OUT BEHIND THE BARN
by Bruce Carlson .... paperback $9.95
TRAINS WEST
by Carole Johnston .... paperback $9.95
KID MONEY (how little bitty kids can earn money)
by Bev Faaborg .... paperback $5.95

MIDWESTERN BOOKS

A FIELD GUIDE TO THE MIDWEST'S WORST RESTAURANTS
by Bruce Carlson .... paperback $5.95
THE MOTORIST'S FIELD GUIDE TO MIDWESTERN FARM EQUIPMENT
(misguided information as only a city slicker can give it)
by Bruce Carlson .... paperback $7.95
VACANT LOT, SCHOOL YARD & BACK ALLEY GAMES OF THE
MIDWEST YEARS AGO
by various authors .... paperback $9.95
MIDWEST SMALL TOWN COOKING
by Bruce Carlson .... (3x5) paperback $5.95
THE BEST OF THE MISSISSIPPI RIVER GHOST STORIES
by Bruce Carlson .... paperback $9.95
HITCHHIKING THE UPPER MIDWEST
by Bruce Carlson .... paperback $7.95
101 WAYS FOR MIDWESTERNERS TO "DO IN" THEIR NEIGHBOR'S
PESKY DOG WITHOUT GETTING CAUGHT
by Bruce Carlson .... paperback $5.95
THE LI'L RED BOOK OF FISHIN' TIPS
by Tom Whitecloud .... paperback $7.95
ANIMAL PESTS & HOW TO GET THE UPPER HAND ON 'EM
by S. Meyer .... paperback $9.95
THE ROAD AIRPLANE KILL COOKBOOK
by Bruce Carlson .... paperback $7.95
OUT BEHIND THE BARN
by Bruce Carlson .... paperback $9.95
TRAINS WEST
by Carole Johnston .... paperback $9.95
KID MONEY (how little bitty kids can earn money)
by Bev Faaborg .... paperback $5.95

RIVER BOOKS

ON THE SHOULDERS OF A GIANT
by M. Cody & D. Walker .... paperback $9.95
THE LI'L RED BOOK OF FISHIN' TIPS
by Tom Whitecloud .... paperback $7.95
SKUNK RIVER ANTHOLOGY
by Gene "Will" Olson .... paperback $9.95

JACK KING vs. DETECTIVE MACKENZIE
 by Netha Bell .... paperback $9.95
THE BEST OF THE MISSISSIPPI RIVER GHOST STORIES
 by Bruce Carlson .... paperback $9.95
LOST & BURIED TREASURES ALONG THE MISSISSIPPI
 by Netha Bell & Gary Scholl .... paperback $9.95
MISSISSIPPI RIVER PO' FOLK
 by Pat Wallace .... paperback $9.95
STRANGE FOLKS ALONG THE MISSISSIPPI
 by Pat Wallace .... paperback $9.95
GHOSTS OF THE OHIO RIVER (from Pittsburgh to Cincinnati)
 by Bruce Carlson .... paperback $9.95
GHOSTS OF THE OHIO RIVER (from Cincinnati to Louisville)
 by Bruce Carlson .... paperback $9.95
TALL TALES OF THE MISSISSIPPI RIVER
 by Dan Titus .... paperback $9.95
TALL TALES OF THE MISSOURI RIVER
 by Dan Titus .... paperback $9.95
TALES OF HACKETT'S CREEK (1940s Mississippi River kids)
 by Dan Titus .... paperback $9.95
101 WAYS TO USE A DEAD RIVER FLY
 by Bruce Carlson .... paperback $7.95
LET'S US GO DOWN TO THE RIVER 'N . . .
 by various authors .... paperback $9.95
LOST & BURIED TREASURE OF THE MISSOURI
 by Netha Bell .... paperback $9.95

COOKBOOKS

ROARING 20s COOKBOOK
 by Bruce Carlson .... paperback $11.95
DEPRESSION COOKBOOK
 by Bruce Carlson .... paperback $11.95
LAKES COUNTRY COOKBOOK
 by Bruce Carlson .... paperback $11.95
A COOKBOOK FOR THEM WHAT AIN'T DONE A LOT OF COOKIN'
 by Bruce Carlson .... paperback $11.95
FLAT-OUT DIRT-CHEAP COOKIN' COOKBOOK
 by Bruce Carlson .... paperback $11.95
APHRODISIAC COOKING
 by Bruce Carlson .... paperback $11.95
WILD CRITTER COOKBOOK
 by Bruce Carlson .... paperback $11.95
I GOT FUNNER-THINGS-TO-DO-THAN COOKIN' COOKBOOK
 by Louise Lum .... paperback $11.95
MISSISSIPPI RIVER COOKIN' BOOK
 by Bruce Carlson .... paperback $11.95
HUNTING IN THE NUDE COOKBOOK
 by Bruce Carlson .... paperback $9.95
DAKOTA COOKIN'
 by Bruce Carlson .... (3x5) paperback $5.95

IOWA COOKIN'
by Bruce Carlson .... (3x5) paperback $5.95
MICHIGAN COOKIN'
by Bruce Carlson .... (3x5) paperback $5.95
MINNESOTA COOKIN'
by Bruce Carlson .... (3x5) paperback $5.95
MISSOURI COOKIN'
by Bruce Carlson .... (3x5) paperback $5.95
ILLINOIS COOKIN'
by Bruce Carlson .... (3x5) paperback $5.95
WISCONSIN COOKIN'
by Bruce Carlson .... (3x5) paperback $5.95
NEW YORK COOKING
by Bruce Carlson .... (3x5) paperback $5.95
PENNSYLVANIA COOKING
by Bruce Carlson .... (3x5) paperback $5.95
OHIO COOKING
by Bruce Carlson .... (3x5) paperback $5.95
KANSAS COOKING
by Bruce Carlson .... (3x5) paperback $5.95
INDIANA COOKING
by Bruce Carlson .... (3x5) paperback $5.95
HILL COUNTRY COOKIN'
by Bruce Carlson .... (3x5) paperback $5.95
MIDWEST SMALL TOWN COOKIN'
by Bruce Carlson .... (3x5) paperback $5.95
APHRODISIAC COOKIN'
by Bruce Carlson .... (3x5) paperback $5.95
PREGNANT LADY COOKIN'
by Bruce Carlson .... (3x5) paperback $5.95
GOOD COOKIN' FROM THE PLAIN PEOPLE
by Bruce Carlson .... (3x5) paperback $5.95
WORKING GIRL COOKING
by Bruce Carlson .... (3x5) paperback $5.95
COOKING FOR ONE
by Barb Layton .... paperback $11.95
SUPER SIMPLE COOKING
by Barb Layton .... (3x5) paperback $5.95
OFF TO COLLEGE COOKBOOK
by Barb Layton .... (3x5) paperback $5.95
COOKING WITH THINGS THAT GO SPLASH
by Bruce Carlson .... (3x5) paperback $5.95
COOKING WITH THINGS THAT GO MOO
by Bruce Carlson .... (3x5) paperback $5.95
COOKING WITH SPIRITS
by Bruce Carlson .... (3x5) paperback $5.95
INDIAN COOKING COOKBOOK
by Bruce Carlson .... paperback $9.95
DIAL-A-DREAM COOKBOOK
by Bruce Carlson .... paperback $11.95
HORMONE HELPER COOKBOOK .... paperback $11.95

CHERRIES! CHERRIES! CHERRIES!
Lisa Nafziger .... (3x5) paperback $5.95
BERRIES! BERRIES! BERRIES!
by Melissa Mosley .... (3x5) paperback $5.95
PUMPKINS! PUMPKINS! PUMPKINS!
by Bruce Carlson .... (3x5) paperback $5.95
PEACHES! PEACHES! PEACHES!
by Melissa Mosley .... (3x5) paperback $5.95
CITRUS! CITRUS! CITRUS!
by Lisa Nafziger .... (3x5) paperback $5.95
APPLES! APPLES! APPLES!
by Lisa Nafziger .... (3x5) paperback $5.95
NUTS! NUTS! NUTS!
Melissa Mosley .... (3x5) paperback $5.95
THE ORCHARDS, BERRY PATCHES & GARDENS COOKBOOK
by Bruce Carlson .... paperback $11.95
KIDS' GARDEN FUN BOOK
.... paperback $5.95
THE ADAPTABLE APPLE
K. McIlquhann .... paperback $9.95
THE BODY SHOP (a lowfat cookbook)
by Sherill Wolff .... paperback $14.95
THE BACK-TO-THE-SUPPER-TABLE COOKBOOK
(a cookbook to rebuild family togetherness)
by Susie Babbington .... paperback $11.95
COOKIN' IN THE GARDEN STATE
by Bruce Carlson .... (3x5) paperback $5.95
WIL-KON-GE INIZAN 'IGANS
(Ojibwa for "to-have-a-feast cooking recipes)
by Tom Whitecloud .... paperback $9.95
KID COOKIN'
by Bev Faaborg .... (3x5) paperback $5.95

MISCELLANEOUS BOOKS

DEAR TABBY (letters to and from a feline advice columnist)
by Bruce Carlson .... paperback $5.95
HOW TO BEHAVE (etiquette advice for non-traditional and awkward circum-
stances such as attending dogfights, what to do when your blind date turns out to
be your spouse, etc.)
by Bruce Carlson .... paperback $5.95
REVENGE OF THE ROADKILL
by Bruce Carlson .... paperback $7.95

POTATOES

Overcooked potatoes can become soggy when the milk is added. Sprinkle with dry powdered milk for the fluffiest mashed potatoes ever.

To hurry up baked potatoes, boil in salted water for 10 minutes, then place in a very hot oven. Or, cut potatoes in half and place them face down on a baking sheet in the oven to make the baking time shorter.

When making potato pancakes, add a little sour cream to keep potatoes from discoloring.

Save some of the water in which the potatoes were boiled - add to some powdered milk and use when mashing. This restores some of the nutrients that were lost in the cooking process.

Use a couple of tablespoons of cream cheese in place of butter for your potatoes; try using sour cream instead of milk when mashing.

ONIONS

To avoid tears when peeling onions, peel them under cold water or refrigerate before chopping.

For sandwiches to go in lunchboxes, sprinkle with dried onion. They will have turned into crisp pieces by lunchtime.

Peel and quarter onions. Place one layer deep in a pan and freeze. Quickly pack in bags or containers while frozen. Use as needed, chopping onions while frozen, with a sharp knife.

TOMATOES

Keep tomatoes in storage with stems pointed downward and they will retain their freshness longer.

Sunlight doesn't ripen tomatoes. It's the warmth that makes them ripen. So find a warm spot near the stove or dishwasher where they can get a little heat.

Save the juice from canned tomatoes in ice cube trays. When frozen, store in plastic bags in freezer for cooking use or for tomato drinks.

To improve the flavor of inexpensive tomato juice, pour a 46-ounce can of it into a refrigerator jar and add one chopped green onion and a cut-up stalk of celery.

A GREAT ENERGY SAVER
When you're near the end of the baking time, turn the oven off and keep the door closed. The heat will stay the same long enough to finish baking your cake or pie and you'll save all that energy.

GRATING CHEESE
Chill the cheese before grating and it will take much less time.

SPECIAL LOOKING PIES
Give a unique look to your pies by using pinking shears to cut the dough. Make a pinked lattice crust!

REMOVING HAM RIND
Before placing ham in the roasting pan, slit rind lengthwise on the underside. The rind will peel away as the ham cooks, and can be easily removed.

SLUGGISH CATSUP
Push a drinking straw to the bottom of the bottle and remove. This admits enough air to start the catsup flowing.

UNMOLDING GELATIN
Rinse the mold pan in cold water and coat with salad oil. The oil will give the gelatin a nice luster and it will easily fall out of the mold.

LEFTOVER SQUASH
Squash that is leftover can be improved by adding some maple syrup before reheated.

NO-SPILL CUPCAKES
An ice cream scoop can be used to fill cupcake papers without spilling.

SLICING CAKE OR TORTE
Use dental floss to slice evenly and cleanly through a cake or torte - simply stretch a length of the floss taut and press down through the cake.

SHRINKLESS LINKS

Boil sausage links for about 8 minutes before frying and they will shrink less and not break at all. Or, you can roll them lightly in flour before frying.

FROZEN BREAD

Put frozen bread loaves in a clean brown paper bag and place for 5 minutes in a 325° oven to thaw completely.

REMOVING THE CORN SILK

Dampen a paper towel or terry cloth and brush downward on the cob of corn. Every strand should come off.

NUTS

To quickly crack open a large amount of nuts, put in a bag and gently hammer until they are cracked open. Then remove nutmeats with a pick.

If nuts are stale, place them in the oven at 250° and leave them there for 5 to 10 minutes. The heat will revive them.

PREVENTING BOIL-OVERS

Add a lump of butter or a few teaspoons of cooking oil to the water. Rice, noodles or spaghetti will not boil over or stick together.

SOFTENING BUTTER

Soften butter quickly by grating it. Or heat a small pan and place it upside-down over the butter dish for several minutes. Or place in the microwave for a few seconds.

MEASURING STICKY LIQUIDS

Before measuring honey or syrup, oil the cup with cooking oil and rinse in hot water.

SCALDED MILK

Add a bit of sugar (without stirring) to milk to prevent it from scorching.

Rinse the pan in cold water before scalding milk, and it will be much easier to clean.

CANNING PEACHES
Don't bother to remove skins when canning or freezing peaches. They will taste better and be more nutritious with the skin on.

ANGEL FOOD COOKIES
Stale angel food cake can be cut into ½-inch slices and shaped with cookie cutters to make delicious "cookies". Just toast in the oven for a few minutes.

HOW TO CHOP GARLIC
Chop in a small amount of salt to prevent pieces from sticking to the knife or chopping board then pulverize with the tip or the knife.

EXCESS FAT ON SOUPS OR STEWS
Remove fat from stews or soups by refrigerating and eliminating fat as it rises and hardens on the surface. Or add lettuce leaves to the pot - the fat will cling to them. Discard lettuce before serving.

BROILED MEAT DRIPPINGS
Place a piece of bread under the rack on which you are broiling meat. Not only will this absorb the dripping fat, but it will reduce the chance of the fat catching on fire.

FAKE SOUR CREAM
To cut down on calories, run cottage cheese through the blender. It can be flavored with chives, extracts, etc., and used in place of mayonnaise.

BROWNED BUTTER
Browning brings out the flavor of the butter, so only half as much is needed for seasoning vegetables if it is browned before it is added.

COOKING DRIED BEANS
When cooking dried beans, add salt after cooking; if salt is added at the start it will slow the cooking process.

TASTY CARROTS
Adding sugar and horseradish to cooked carrots improves their flavor.

EGGS

If you shake the egg and you hear a rattle, you can be sure it's stale. A really fresh egg will float and a stale one will sink.

If you are making deviled eggs and want to slice it perfectly, dip the knife in water first. The slice will be smooth with no yolk sticking to the knife.

The white of an egg is easiest to beat when it's at room temperature. So leave it out of the refrigerator about ½ hour before using it.

To make light and fluffy scrambled eggs, add a little water while beating the eggs.

Add vinegar to the water while boiling eggs. Vinegar helps to seal the egg, since it acts on the calcium in the shell.

To make quick-diced eggs, take your potato masher and go to work on a boiled egg.

If you wrap each egg in aluminum foil before boiling it, the shell won't crack when it's boiling.

To make those eggs go further when making scrambled eggs for a crowd, add a pinch of baking powder and 2 tsp. of water per egg.

A great trick for peeling eggs the easy way - when they are finished boiling, turn off the heat and just let them sit in the pan with the lid on for about 5 minutes. Steam will build up under the shell and they will just fall away.

Or, quickly rinse hot hard-boiled eggs in cold water, and the shells will be easier to remove.

When you have saved a lot of egg yolks from previous recipes; use them in place of whole eggs for baking or thickening. Just add 2 yolks for every whole egg.

Fresh or hard-boiled? Spin the egg. If it wobbles, it is raw - if it spins easily, it's hard-boiled.

Add a few drops of vinegar to the water when poaching an egg to keep it from running all over the pan.

Add 1 T. of water per egg white to increase the quantity of beaten egg white when making meringue.

Try adding eggshells to coffee after it has perked, for a better flavor.

CARROT MARINADE
Marinate carrot sticks in dill pickle juice.

CLEAN CUKES
A ball of nylon net cleans and smooths cucumbers when making pickles.

FRESH GARLIC
Peel garlic and store in a covered jar of vegetable oil. The garlic will stay fresh and the oil will be nicely flavored for salad dressings.

LEFTOVER WAFFLES
Freeze waffles that are left; they can be reheated in the toaster.

FLUFFY RICE
Rice will be fluffier and whiter if you add 1 tsp. of lemon juice to each quart of water.

NUTRITIOUS RICE
Cook rice in liquid saved from cooking vegetables to add flavor and nutrition. A nutty taste can be achieved by adding wheat germ to the rice.

PERFECT NOODLES
When cooking noodles, bring required amount of water to a boil, add noodles, turn heat off and allow to stand for 20 minutes. This prevents overboiling and the chore of stirring. Noodles won't stick to the pan with this method.

EASY CROUTONS
Make delicious croutons for soup or salad by saving toast, cutting into cubes, and sauteeing in garlic butter.

BAKED FISH
To keep fish from sticking to the pan, bake on a bed of chopped onion, celery and parsley. This also adds a nice flavor to the fish.

ROCK-HARD BROWN SUGAR

Add a slice of soft bread to the package of brown sugar, close the bag tightly, and in a few hours the sugar will be soft again. If you need it in a hurry, simply grate the amount called for with a hand grater. Or, put brown sugar and a cup of water (do not add to the sugar, set it alongside of it) in a covered pan. Place in the oven (low heat) for awhile. Or, buy liquid brown sugar.

THAWING FROZEN MEAT

Seal the meat in a plastic bag and place in a bowl of very warm water. Or, put in a bag and let cold water run over it for an hour or so.

CAKED OR CLOGGED SALT

Tightly wrap a piece of aluminum foil around the salt shaker. This will keep the dampness out of the salt. To prevent clogging, keep 5 to 10 grains of rice inside your shaker.

SOGGY POTATO CHIPS, CEREAL AND CRACKERS

If potato chips lose their freshness, place under broiler for a few moments. Care must be taken not to brown them. You can crisp soggy cereal and crackers by putting them on a cookie sheet and heating for a few minutes in the oven.

PANCAKE SYRUP

To make an inexpensive syrup for pancakes, save small amounts of leftover jams and jellies in a jar. Or, fruit-flavored syrup can be made by adding 2 C. sugar to 1 C. of any kind of fruit juice and cooking until it boils.

EASY TOPPING

A good topping for gingerbread, coffeecake, etc., can easily be made by freezing the syrup from canned fruit and adding 1 T. of butter and 1 T. of lemon juice to 2 C. of syrup. Heat until bubbly, and thicken with 2 T. of flour.

TASTY CHEESE SANDWICHES

Toast cheese sandwiches in a frying pan lightly greased with bacon fat for a delightful new flavor.

HURRY-UP HAMBURGERS

Poke a hole in the middle of the patties while shaping them. The burgers will cook faster and the holes will disappear when done.

TENDERIZING MEAT
Boiled meat: Add a tablespoon of vinegar to the cooking water.

Tough meat or game: Make a marinade of equal parts cooking vinegar and heated bouillon. Marinate for 2 hours.

Steak: Simply rub in a mixture of cooking vinegar and oil. Allow to stand for 2 hours.

Chicken: To stew an old hen, soak it in vinegar for several hours before cooking. It will taste like a spring chicken.

INSTANT WHITE SAUCE
Blend together 1 C. soft butter and 1 C. flour. Spread in an ice cube tray, chill well, cut into 16 cubes before storing in a plastic bag in the freezer. For medium-thick sauce, drop 1 cube into 1 C. of milk and heat slowly, stirring as it thickens.

UNPLEASANT COOKING ODORS
While cooking vegetables that give off unpleasant odors, simmer a small pan of vinegar on top of the stove. Or, add vinegar to the cooking water. To remove the odor of fish from cooking and serving implements, rinse in vinegar water.

DON'T LOSE THOSE VITAMINS
Put vegetables in water after the water boils - not before - to be sure to preserve all the vegetables' vitamins.

CLEAN AND DEODORIZE YOUR CUTTING BOARD
Bleach it clean with lemon juice. Take away strong odors like onion with baking soda. Just rub in.

KEEP THE COLOR IN BEETS
If you find that your beets tend to lose color when you boil them, add a little lemon juice.

NO-SMELL CABBAGE
Two things to do to keep cabbage smell from filling the kitchen; don't overcook it (keep it crisp) and put half a lemon in the water when you boil it.

NON-STICKING BACON
Roll a package of bacon into a tube before opening. This will loosen the slices and keep them from sticking together.

TASTY HOT DOGS
Boil hot dogs in sweet pickle juice and a little water for a different tate.

GOLDEN-BROWN CHICKEN
For golden-brown fried chicken, roll it in powdered milk instead of flour.

DOUBLE BOILER HINT
Toss a few marbles in the bottom of a double boiler. When the water boils down, the noise will let you know!

FLOUR PUFF
Keep a powder puff in your flour container to easily dust your rolling pin or pastry board.

JAR LABELS
Attach canning labels to the lids instead of the sides of jelly jars, to prevent the chore of removing the labels when the contents are gone.

DIFFERENT MEATBALLS
Try using crushed corn flakes or corn bread instead of bread crumbs in a meatball recipe or use onion-flavored potato chips.

BLENDER
Fill part way with hot water and add a drop of detergent. Cover and turn it on for a few seconds. Rinse and drain dry.

BREADBOARDS
To rid cutting board of onion, garlic or fish smell, cut a lime or lemon in two and rub the surface with the cut side of the fruit.

Or, make a paste of baking soda and water and apply generously. Rinse.

COPPER POTS
Fill a spray bottle with vinegar and add 3 T. of salt. Spray solution liberally on copper pot. Let set for awhile, then simply rub clean.

Dip lemon halves in salt and rub.

Or, rub with Worcestershire sauce or catsup. The tarnish will disappear.

Clean with toothpaste and rinse.

BURNT AND SCORCHED PANS
Sprinkle burnt pans liberally with baking soda, adding just enough water to moisten. Let stand for several hours. You can generally lift the burned portions right out of the pan.

Stubborn stains on non-stick cookware can be removed by boiling 2 T. of baking soda, ½ C. vinegar, and 1 C. water for 10 minutes. Re-season with salad oil.

CAST-IRON SKILLETS
Clean the outside of the pan with commercial oven cleaner. Let set for 2 hours and the accumulated black stains can be removed with vinegar and water.

CAN OPENER
Loosen grime by brushing with an old toothbrush. To thoroughly clean blades, run a paper towel through the cutting process.